MAKING SACRED

Spirituality for the Lay Person

Betty McConville

A GRAIL PUBLICATION

1992

© 1992 The Grail (England)

First published 1992
ISBN 0 901829 80 3

Cover design: Ann Dawson
Calligraphy: Philippa Craig

Published by The Grail, 125 Waxwell Lane,
Pinner, Middx HA5 3ER

Distributed by: Gracewing/Fowler Wright
Unit 2, Southern Avenue,
Leominster, Herefords HR6 0QF

Printed in Great Britain by
Billings & Sons Ltd, Worcester

CONTENTS

Page

v	Introduction
ix	Spirituality of the Laity
12	Called to Become
15	Lay Life
23	Spirituality of Work
35	Network of Relationships
43	Prayer
51	In the Darkness
59	Creation Spirituality
69	Our Journey
77	Evangelisation
85	Justice and Peace
93	Mary - Mother of the Church
99	Spirituality of Sexuality
108	Appendix A: Ways into Prayer
110	Appendix B: Supplementary material
113	Appendix C: Suggested Hymns
116	Acknowledgements Bibliography

INTRODUCTION

The purpose of these sessions is to help people to look at their own personal spirituality. The aim is to lead towards inward reflection on personal experiences of daily living, rather than inviting discussion *about* prayer and spirituality.

To this end, each meeting has a short article by way of introduction to start people thinking about a particular aspect of spirituality. The second section provides points for each person's personal reflection. Then follows a period for people to share something of their reflection. The final section provides a short prayer-time on the theme of the meeting, giving the opportunity for praying together as a group.

Each section is arranged to be as flexible as possible so that the organiser can suit the session to the group. The meetings may be used as single one-off occasions or as a series. Choose which topics would seem most suitable for the people you wish to bring together.

There is no set pattern on how this material should be used. However, the following is suggested as a guide for anyone planning a session:

a) A period of 1½ - 2 hours will be needed if the plan of the session described above is used.

b) The leader should study the material provided at the beginning of the meeting and decide how best to get this over to the group in order to stimulate thought and lead to reflection. Ideally, the material could be presented in the leader's own words in the form of a short introduction. Sometimes, it is helpful to write up key words from each section as you go along, eg using the headings given. Alternatively, after the introduction, the leader could give a copy of the material to each person; or arrange for people to read different sections aloud.

c) Each person is then asked to be silent and reflect on their own lives in relation to the particular aspect of spirituality presented in the session. If it is possible for people to find a place to be on their own, it would be ideal; but otherwise they remain in silence in the room. A period of 15 - 20 minutes is recommended.

The members of the group are then asked to share something of their reflection. It is important to stress that there is no obligation to share everything - it is entirely up to them to share what they feel comfortable with or what seems appropriate. The leader will need to decide whether to divide the group into 3's or 4's, or to remain one large group. If divided, then it is recommended that there be a short period of 'coming together' before moving on to the prayer-time.

d) We have stressed that the sessions are intended to lead to personal reflection and sharing rather than to discussion. However, unless the group is comfortable about sharing in a more reflective way, there may be a tendency for the session to become a discussion, with perhaps the more confident members talking a great deal and the shyer ones being silent. To avoid this, it may be a good plan to give a few hints to the group on how best to proceed in their sharing.

The following may be helpful:

1. Be sure to listen to each person.

2. Allow everyone a chance to speak if they wish to do so.

3. Remember that it is an exchange of your own experiences so try to speak for yourself using 'I...' rather than 'They....'.

4. Above all, respond with encouragement and support when a person has shared.

If, however, the group is made up of people who have difficulty with the content of the meetings, or are confused by the approach, it may be best to allow for discussion and clarification for at least some of the time, and treat it as a learning session.

e) In order to end the meeting in a reflective manner, a prayer-time is provided. Again, this may be used in as flexible a way as possible. You may wish to introduce readings other than the ones suggested. The same might apply to the hymns.

Each prayer-time includes some symbolic activity or gesture, to allow for involvement and participation of each person present. How this is done will obviously depend on the situation; but since it does give emphasis to the purpose of the meeting, and symbols can express spiritual ideas far better than words, it would clearly be helpful if some aspect of it is carried out.

It is important for lay people to gain confidence in preparing suitable liturgies which are relevant to their own lives and which can be celebrated on various occasions.

Finally, I would emphasise that the sessions are concerned with lay spirituality in the secular world, and that their purpose is not directly about parish life or the church as an institution. It is always easier to talk in general terms than to reflect on one's own situation, so it is important to try to keep the reflections on a personal level, and the sharing specific and concrete in terms of people's own experience.

You will discover, throughout this book, short prayers and sayings from various sources. These may be helpful for individuals to use as a basis for their personal prayer, or they may be used as additional or alternative material to the sessions.

SPIRITUALITY OF THE LAITY

Following the Synod of Catholic Bishops in 1987, a summary of the discussions was published in the document **'Christifideles Laici'**. This was simplified by the Grail under the title of **'This is the Laity'**.

While most of the document is concerned with the laity's involvement and participation in society and in the church, there are constant reminders that underlying all mission must be a deep spirituality and prayer life. As the characteristic feature of the laity is its secularity, then this spirituality needs to be expressed within secular life.

Whilst spirituality is the same for everyone, lay people are being urged to discover a spirituality which can be lived out in the context of everyday life.

> *So far as the laity are concerned,*
> *the place where God calls them to work*
> *is in the world around them,*
> *in their ordinary life and work,*
> *and in their relationships...*
> *So the world becomes the place*
> *and the means*
> *whereby the laity fulfil their vocation...*
>
> *The primary vocation of the laity*
> *is to become holy people.*
>   This is the Laity, Nos. 15 & 16

The Bishops suggest that it is up to the laity themselves to work out this 'secular spirituality' by sharing with one another and encouraging one another.

I am a member of the Grail Secular Institute, a form of dedicated life in the Church whereby the members remain lay and involved in the secular activities in the world. In response to the promptings of the Holy Spirit, these Institutes emerged in the Catholic Church precisely to bear witness to the importance of making secular society sacred.

It seems an appropriate task for the Grail to put together this book to enable lay people to consider different aspects of their lives, and share their experiences and spiritual journeys. I have tried to keep the material 'down to earth' and related to what I perceive to be the issues facing many people in their lives. I have no doubt there are other aspects I have missed out, but I would hope that people will not follow these sessions too slavishly, but will adapt them to meet their own needs.

Although the idea for this book has sprung from the document **'Christifideles Laici'** produced by Catholic Bishops, and uses some extracts from it in the material, I think Christians from other churches will find most of the issues totally applicable to themselves. And I would stress to Catholic users that this is not a commentary on the document, and is not concerned directly with lay roles in the parish.

*

To give some idea of my approach to spirituality for lay people, I have tried to give emphasis to these aspects of lay spirituality:

* Lay spirituality is characterised by the integration of prayer into everyday life.

* It is having an awareness of God's presence in the midst of all experiences, encounters and activities.

* It is a spirituality to do with *BECOMING*, in becoming the person God wants us to be.

* It is therefore concerned with the whole person and with each person's human growth and development.

* It is a way in which a person, having within them the living presence of the Spirit, acts and responds according to his or her characteristic gifts and insights.

* It is a spirituality which emphasises service to others, and involvement in the strivings and sufferings of the whole of humanity.

* It is concerned with the *BECOMING* of the whole of creation, and the protection and development of our environment and the cosmic planet.

* It is a spirituality which leads to mission and being salt and leaven in secular society, working with others to further God's Kingdom.

* As members of the Christian community, our personal spirituality is united with that of the whole Church through its liturgical and sacramental life.

* Above all, it is a spirituality of hope and sure knowledge of the victory of the resurrection and glory which is to come.

CALLED TO BECOME

You are called to become
A perfect creation.
No one is called to become
Who you are called to be.
It does not matter
How short or tall
Or thick-set or slow
You may be.
It does not matter
Whether you sparkle with life
Or are silent as a still pool;
Whether you sing your song aloud
Or weep alone in darkness.
It does not matter
Whether you feel loved and admired,
Or unloved and alone.
For you are called to become
A perfect creation.
No one's shadow
should cloud your becoming.
No one's light
should dispel your spark.
For the Lord delights in you,

Jealously looks upon you
And encourages with gentle joy
Every movement of the Spirit
Within you.
Unique and loved you stand,
Beautiful or stunted in your growth
But never without hope and life.
For you are called to become
A perfect creation.
This becoming may be
Gentle or harsh,
Subtle or violent,
But it never ceases,
Never pauses or hesitates,
Only is -
Creative force -
Calling you,
Calling you to become
A perfect creation.

    Edwina Gately
   Psalms of a Laywoman

HOLINESS
HAS TO
DO
WITH
VERY
ORDINARY
THINGS.
Ruth Burrows

LAY LIFE

Spirituality simply means following Christ. For lay people this means following Christ in the context of the secular. 'This is the Laity' says:

> The primary vocation of lay people
> is to become holy.
> And the world
> becomes the place and means
> of holiness.   Para 15

Thus it is essential to find a spirituality which directs us towards the world, and in which we allow ourselves to be caught up in God's work in the world. First, let us look at some of the trends which have influenced our thoughts about spirituality and holiness.

Sacred and Secular

From the early centuries, the church has been strongly influenced by what was originally Greek thought, which looked at human beings and the world in a dual way, by making a split between soul/body, sacred/secular, spiritual/temporal, humanity/creation. The result was to view the soul as somehow separate from the body. The soul had to be preserved from the danger of being led astray and hindered in its spiritual growth by our human side and by worldly things. This led to a spirituality which tended to be very personal and pious, inward looking, concerned about guilt, religious in outlook and language, and far removed from daily life.

> The split between the faith
> which many profess

and their daily lives
deserves to be counted among
the more serious errors of our age.   Para 59

Monasticism

Over the centuries, another great influence on spirituality has been the model of monasticism. So many of the great saints have emerged from this way of life that it is understandable that these outstanding spiritual figures have influenced us and continue to do so. Many religious orders, even the most active, have adapted forms of the monastic life, and this spirituality has tended to influence much of the teaching and preaching about prayer and the spiritual life in the church.

What are some of the elements of monasticism? Apartness, stability, celibacy, obedience to the rule and order of day, silence, community, regular prayer, authority, a balanced life of prayer, work, and recreation. The monastic life is a sign to the world of the transcendent, of God's Kingdom. But, however inspiring such a way of life is, it cannot form the basis - even in a modified form - of a spirituality for lay people whose lives differ so fundamentally in every way. We need to find a spirituality which can be lived out with confidence and serenity in a secular situation.

Being Whole

Today, there are new influences which affect our attitudes. This generation has had the insights of psychology, the human growth movement, and the behavioural sciences, as well as influences of Eastern spirituality. These have taught us that the human person cannot be divided into soul and body, or any other way. We have come to understand that body, mind, spirit, emotions, sexuality, all make up the whole person, and are inter-related. Other influences help us to recognise that all life is a gift from God, and the human person is the wonder of God's creativity. As St Ireneas said, in the third century: 'The glory of God is the glory of a person fully alive.' So we can rejoice in our humanity, and in the whole of creation. The development and growth of ourselves as individuals is part of our spirituality.

Spirituality is to do with *BECOMING*, of becoming the person God wants us to be. We each have our own journey through life, our own history, our own circumstances, joys and difficulties. We can be very happy in the knowledge that God is intimately involved and concerned with each one of us.

Using what the world offers

We are asked to become holy using the means which the world offers. The 'means' are the things which make up our lives: our work, our relationships, our activities, our leisure time. It is essential, of course, to find time and space to devote to God in direct and explicit prayer or meditation, as did Christ himself when he went apart to pray to his heavenly Father. But, as Christians, we know that the Spirit of God is with us at all times and in all places, whether we are consciously aware of it or not. Our task is to become more open and more in touch with this divine life working within us.

Sometimes, we may become aware of special moments of grace which can truly be called experiences of God. Generally, we know only by faith that God is with us in these experiences and events in life: in the way we relate to people, our families and friends; how we deal with different situations; how we try to prompt the good in our work and everyday life; how we strive to bring about a just and compassionate society. In other words, how we bring Christ into our sphere of influence, and minister to others. Prayer and ministry cannot be separated. Prayer leads us to be much more aware and sensitive to the needs of society, and in turn, these needs lead us to prayer.

Praying with the Church

We are emphasising the importance of a personal spirituality, yet we are also members of a praying community of believers. We share in the priesthood of Christ and, as lay people, we offer to God all our daily activities, through our personal offering and alongside the offering of others.

Many people use the Morning and Evening Prayer of the Church for this reason. In the Eucharist, the laity's contribution is to bring their experiences of the secular world to the altar, and help to celebrate a liturgy which is relevant and concerns the issues of the day. This enables the priest to celebrate sacramentally the ordinary experiences of the laity; and he, in turn, enables the laity to fulfil their vocation and ministry by being strengthened and revitalised by the liturgy.

Personal Reflection

1   How do I try to help myself become aware of God in the activities of daily life?

2   What are the things which hinder me and make it difficult to be as aware of God as I would like?

3   Are there occasions which seem to be special moments of grace when I experience God in everyday situations?

4. Every stage in one's life journey brings its potential for growth and renewal. What issues are there for me now?

Prayer-Time

Preparation: Prepare a small coffee table with a suitable symbol - eg a candle, crucifix, and flowers - as a focal point of the liturgy. Also, place a small dish or basket on the table. Provide, for each person, a piece of paper and a pencil which will be needed during the liturgy.

Introduction: We gather together to praise and honour the One who comes, Christ Jesus, who makes himself present in our midst through the power of the Holy Spirit.

The Church exists in the world to continue Christ's work, which concerns the saving of humanity and the renewal of the whole world. The world then becomes the place whereby we fulfil our vocation. We are called to sanctify the world by being within it like salt, like leaven, to show Christ to others.

Reading: Matthew 5, 13-14

You are the salt of the earth; but if salt has lost its taste, how shall its saltness be restored? It is no longer good for anything except to be thrown out and trodden underfoot by everyone. You are the light of the world. A city set on a hill cannot be hid. Nor do people light a lamp and put it under a bushel, but on a stand, and it gives light to all in the house. Let your light so shine before everyone, that they may see your good works and give glory to your Father who is in heaven.

All: Psalm 120

I lift up my eyes to the mountains,
from where shall come my help?
My help shall come from the Lord,
who made heaven and earth.

> May he never allow you to stumble!
> Let him sleep not, your guard!
> No, he sleeps not, nor slumbers,
> Israel's guard!
>
> The Lord is your guard and your shade;
> at your right side he stands.
> By day the sun shall not smite you,
> nor the moon in the night.
>
> The Lord will guard you from evil,
> he will guard your soul.
> The Lord will guard your going and coming
> both now and for ever.

Spirituality is the way a person, having within them the living presence of the Holy Spirit, acts and responds according to his or her characteristic gifts and insights. God works through each of us, making use of our personalities, and our own special gifts and qualities. Reflect, in silence, about your own particular gifts and strengths.

(Each person is given a piece of paper and a pencil, and asked to write down a gift which they know God has given them, and which can be used for the benefit of others. Fold the piece of paper, and place it in the dish provided, on the table.)

Prayer

> Lord, we thank you for these gifts
> and qualities which you have given
> to each person here. May we use
> them generously and with confid-
> ence, in the service of others, and
> in building up the community.

Reading: 1 Cor 12, 4-7

Now, there are varieties of gifts, but the same Spirit; and there are varieties of service, but the same Lord; and there are varieties of working, but it is the same God who inspires them all in everyone. To each is given the manifestation of the Spirit for the common good.

All: Say together the Grail Prayer

> Lord Jesus,
> I give you my hands
> to do your work.
> I give you my feet
> to go your way.
> I give you my eyes
> to see as you do.
> I give you my tongue
> to speak your words.
> I give you my mind
> that you may think in me.
> I give you my spirit
> that you may pray in me.
> Above all, I give you my heart,
> that you may love in me
> your Father and all the world.
> I give you my whole self
> that you may grow in me.
> So that it is you, Lord Jesus,
> who live and work and pray in me.
>   Amen

HYMN: Choose one which reflects the theme of the liturgy. See suggestions at the back.

Bidding Prayers: if desired.

Final Prayer: These words are by Dag Hammarskjöld, who was an outstanding layman working in the world of the United Nations. He was an intensely dedicated public servant, who drew strength from his sense of communion with God. His writings constitute one of the most important spiritual documents of our time.

Have mercy upon us.
Have mercy upon our efforts, that we,
Before thee, in love and faith,
Righteousness and humility,
May follow thee, with self-denial,
Steadfastness and courage,
And meet thee in silence.
Give us a pure heart,
That we may see thee,
A humble heart that we may hear thee,
A heart of love that we may serve thee,
A heart of faith that we may live thee.
Amen

SPIRITUALITY OF WORK

Whether in paid employment or simply looking after our homes, families, other people, work is an essential way of fulfilling our vocation and continuing Christ's mission on earth.

As Christians, we believe that God created the world and, having done so, in the words of Genesis 'God saw that it was good'. We believe in the essential goodness of the world and of the whole of creation. One of the truths of revelation is that men and women, by their work, share in the continuing work of the Creator. We know that, by working at the most ordinary of activities, we are furthering human progress and the good of the human family.

Becoming Human

Work is an invaluable means of fulfilling ourselves and of reaching beyond ourselves to others. We are especially fortunate if the work we do makes full use of our gifts and resources, and enables us to grow and develop.

Through our work we are also contributing to the progress and development of society. Human achievement and progress in no way diminishes God's power and involvement. They are part of his plan, and a sign of his Spirit working in us and through us.

Complexities of modern life

It was probably easier for those who lived in an earlier agricultural society to be in touch with God, and feel their dependence on him in relation to their work. We live in a more complex world: in an industrial, technical and scientific age, and in a fiercely competitive market economy where success and profit-making are all important. It is difficult for the individual to feel they have a personal part to play.

Even work which is directed to the service of people, as in education, medicine and the social services, exists in the context of vast agencies and administrative units, However, this is the world in which we find ourselves, this is the situation we are in: full of problems and difficulties, needing people of integrity and compassion with a vision of God's purpose for humanity.

Employment

Through work, we earn the money to provide for ourselves or our families, to bring security and provide a quality of life which can be enjoyed. Money is essential for our national economy. Money is a return for our labour and skills and, as such, we can take pride in it and see it as a reward for our work and talents. We all know that there can be a tendency to become too ambitious, when money and possessions can become an end in themselves. We need to bear in mind that what we *are* is far more important than our success or achievements.

Alongside paid employment, there are all the everyday domestic tasks which involve most people, as well as the care of families and dependants. There are also many voluntary activities which provide a service to those in need, as well as the sharing of skills and interests for personal enjoyment and community entertainment.

The Cross

Work is not a punishment, but an opportunity to

share in God's creativity. However, work does involve effort, and even the most satisfying of jobs can have elements of drudgery, frustration and sheer hard slog. There are some jobs which are extremely boring and routine, and yet this is how many people have to earn a living.

Often, people may suffer disappointment and feel resentment because they are not achieving the hoped-for success or recognition. For some, domestic work, caring for children or elderly relatives can seem at times difficult and restrictive. When we experience work as hard, unrewarding or unsatisfying, we may consciously unite this hardship with Christ's suffering; and be comforted by the fact that it is through his cross that Christ brought salvation.

Whatever our work may be, our task is to bring the spirit of the Risen Christ into our situation and, in this way, **all** our efforts contribute to the bringing of the Kingdom.

Unemployment

Unemployment is a reality of today's world. It is a tragedy for the individual who suffers the loss of a job, bringing with it feelings of betrayal, the undermining of confidence, and anxiety about the future. Unemployment is experienced by people from all sections of our society, and there are young people who have not had a job after leaving school, or after gaining qualifications.

The Christian community needs to be aware of the terrible effect that being without a job has on the individual person; and, where possible, to try and influence events to ensure that more paid work is available. However, it may be equally necessary to face the fact that, in our modern society, full employment for everyone may not be achievable. The question then arises, how do we arrange our labour force to ensure each person's right to work?

A sense of identity

For most people, work is a means of providing a role in life and giving a sense of personal identity. When asked *who we are*, we may well respond by saying *what we do*. However, it is possible to become obsessive about work, and depend on it too much for giving us a sense of worth and purpose. Work is only one aspect of life, and we need to value ourselves and others for the persons we are. Whilst work is of great importance, it is wrong to feel guilty about leisure. God does not demand constant labour on our part, and there are other ways of 'being' and finding purpose in life.

Retirement and redundancy

There are senior citizens who have looked forward to retirement for years, and have discovered that it is a wonderful new phase in life. But there are others - especially those for whom retirement has come earlier than expected, or who have faced unexpected redundancy, - who suffer profoundly from the loss of work and purpose in life. These feelings and changes in lifestyle can also affect their partners and those close to them.

Many retired people find immense satisfaction in taking on voluntary work of all kinds. Others find new gifts and talents through trying out fresh interests and hobbies. Older people should feel able to enjoy a more leisurely way of life, and not only be free to enjoy these new interests and experiences, but also to nurture a deeper inner life of faith and trust in God.

A means of holiness

Work has intrinsic value in itself and, if our lives are orientated to God, then work becomes a means of holiness. We can be confident that all aspects of our labour are part and parcel of our discipleship of Christ. We can make this explicit by:-

a) making a morning offering: spending some time in prayer before the activities of the day;

b) finding moments during the day when one is able to renew one's commitment:

c) sharing in the Eucharist, when we offer our work and occupations with Christ's own offering to God the Father. We receive the Bread of Life to strengthen us in being a sign of his presence in the secular world, and continuing Christ's work of establishing the Kingdom of God.

Personal Reflection

1   What aspects of my work do I find most creative and life-giving both for myself and for others?

2   How do I see my work in relation to building up the human family and the progress of society?

3   Is it possible for me to recognise that my work is sharing in God's creative power and contributing to his Kingdom on earth?

4   Are there aspects of my working life that I would like to change or develop?

5   How balanced is my life in relation to my work, leisure, personal space for reflection, enjoyment and being with family and friends?

WE
ARE
FELLOW-
 WORKERS
 WITH GOD,
 CO-CREATORS
 IN EVERY-
 THING
 WE DO.
   Meister Eckhart

Prayer-Time

Preparation: During the liturgy, each person will be asked to present something which is a symbolic representation of his or her work, eg: diary, watch, pen, etc. An alternative could be to provide a large sheet of paper on the wall or on the floor, with crayons or markers, and ask the group to make a joint symbolic drawing including each person's work.

Introduction: Lord, we are gathered to listen to your Word, to encourage one another, and to renew our commitment to furthering your Kingdom.

Reading: John 15 vv 5-12, 16

This is part of Jesus' farewell message to his disciples as he sent them out into his vineyard:

> I am the vine, you are the branches. If you remain in me and my words remain in you, you may ask what you will and you shall get it. It is to the glory of my Father that you should bear much fruit, and then you will be my disciples. As the Father has loved me, so I have loved you. Remain in my love. If you keep my commandments, you will remain in my love; just as I have kept my Father's commandments, and remain in his love. I have told you this so that my own joy may be in you, and your joy may be complete.
>
> This is my commandment: Love one another as I have loved you. You did not choose me, I chose you; and I commissioned you to go out and to bear fruit, fruit that will last; and then the Father will give you anything you ask him in my name. What I command you is to love one another.

ALL: Psalm 99

Cry out with joy to the Lord, all the earth,

Serve the Lord with gladness,
Come before him, singing for joy.

Know that he, the Lord, is God.
He made us, we belong to him.
We are his people, the sheep of his flock.

Go within his gates, giving thanks.
Enter his courts with songs of praise.
Give thanks to him and bless his name.

Indeed, how good is the Lord,
eternal his merciful love.
He is faithful from age to age.

Reading: from Cardinal Newman

God has created me
to do him some definite service;
he has committed some work to me
which he has not committed to another.
I have my mission -
I may never know it in this life,
but I shall be told it in the next.
Somehow I am necessary for his purposes;
as necessary in my place
as an Archangel in his.
I have a part in this great work;
I am a link in a chain,
a bond of connection between persons.
He has not created me for naught.
I shall do good, I shall do his work;
I shall be an angel of peace,
a preacher of truth in my own place.
Deign to fulfil your high purposes in me.
I am here to serve you, to be yours,
to be your instrument.

Pause for reflection.

(Here, the group is asked to present symbols of their work: either putting them on the floor, or on a table provided; or, in the case of the drawing, to actually come forward each in turn, and draw the symbol they have chosen, and make it into a group effort.)

Prayer

Lord, take these symbols of our daily work and help us to feel pride in what we are able to achieve, and what we are able to contribute to your Kingdom on earth.

Reading: from 'This is Human Work': para 25

> The best motive for our work is knowing
> that we share in Creation...
> and in our daily lives
> help each other to become holier.
> It calls for each of us
> to work vigorously,
> so that goods created by human work
> should be what the Creator intended.

All:
> Be born in us
> incarnate love
> take our flesh and blood
> give us your humanity;
> take our eyes and
> give us your vision;
> take our minds and
> give us your pure thought;
> take our feet and
> set them in your path;
> take our hands and
> fold them in your prayer;
> take our hearts and
> give them your will
> to love.
>   Caryll Houselander

Bidding Prayers

We are encouraged to develop our attitudes to work. May we pray with confidence:

Lord, may our work develop our creativity,
help us to share our gifts
and give service to others.
Lord, hear us.
Response: Lord, graciously hear us.

We put before you and ask you to bless
all the people with whom we work.
Lord, hear us.
Response:

May we work with enthusiasm
and wholehearted commitment
to furthering your Kingdom on earth.
Lord, hear us.
Response:

Help us to be compassionate and loving
in our service of those in need.
Lord, hear us.
Response:

Show us how to plan our lives
so that we find space for ourselves,
time for those we love,
and opportunity to enjoy the good things of life.
Lord, hear us.
Response:

All: O Lord, we ask you to help us to transform these prayers into deeds; so that your love, by illuminating ours, may bring a world of joy to everyone.
AMEN

Hymn: See Appendix C

> We are fellow-helpers with God,
> co-creators of everything we do.
> When Word and work are returned
> to their source and origin,
> then all work
> is accomplished divinely in God.
> And there, too, the soul loses itself
> in a wonderful enchantment.
> Meister Eckhart

Final Prayer

God be in mine eyes, and in my looking;
God be in my mouth, and in my speaking;
God be in my heart, and in my thinking;
God be at mine end, and at my departing.

O people,
learn
to dance;
otherwise
the angels
in heaven
won't know
what to
do with
you!
— St Augustine

NETWORK OF RELATIONSHIPS

Jesus told his followers 'Love your neighbour as yourself.' We know that one of the most demanding tasks of a Christian is loving others and expressing our love in the context of a whole network of relationships. Spirituality is certainly to do with loving, and our charity must include many different people, but starts with those who are nearest to us.

Married Love

Marriage is perhaps the most intimate and permanent expression of love, because it involves a personal commitment in mutual self-giving. Sexual love expressed within marriage is holy in itself and therefore the source of God's grace and a means of holiness.

Early on in their relationship, husbands and wives learn that the first romantic love has to give place to a deeper love which helps them to be faithful, to accept their differences, to cope with one another's emotional needs, and to face up to the good times and the bad times in their life together. These efforts to grow in love towards each other, in ways which are very ordinary and commonplace, are giving God glory and become a means of growth and holiness.

The love and relationship of one married couple extends to many other people: their own children, their respective families, relatives and friends. One marriage relationship touches a whole network of others, as can be seen from a wedding or anniversary.

Children

The marriage of most couples is blessed by the birth of children. Each new child brought into the world is an expression of God's love and a sign of hope and promise. Indeed, some women have expressed the view that the actual process of giving birth to a baby is one of the most sacred and spiritual moments of their lives, as they feel they are at one with God in bringing a new person into the world.

To ensure the growth and full development of a child requires the constant and unconditional love of parents. As all parents know, this love has often to be expressed in many ways not always understood by the child.

The Family

Early in our lives, we learn how to relate to the rest of the family: brothers and sisters, cousins, etc. Whatever changes may be taking place in our society in regard to the family, the basic needs of people from early childhood to old age remain the same.

We have the need to feel secure, to be loved and accepted as we are, and to be with people who share our values. The family still provides the strongest bond and greatest support for most of us. And Christian family life stands for all that is authentically human, and the manner in which it is lived out is an expression of this belief in the dignity of the human person.

The family provides the place where the most important events of life are remembered and celebrated: baptisms, birthdays, weddings, anniversaries, successes; as well as the great Christian feasts.

Growing To Adulthood

Young people who are becoming independent

have a particular need to be open to God's guidance and to become the person he wants them to be. At this time, they have all the pressures of choosing the right career, discovering new relationships, facing up to the excitements and challenges of a secular world. Many young people reject past values, including religious ones, and go their own way. This is painful for parents and young people alike. Parents often feel they have failed as parents, and feel angry and upset. It is important for them, not only to try and accept what is happening, but also to encourage and praise their children. This is a time of real testing of their relationship.

Adults and Parents

The continuing relationship we have with our parents, as life goes on, can be an important one, from both sides: On the one side, the concern for and care of ageing parents; on the other, the encouragement and support by parents of their adult children, without interfering or undermining their right to choose their own way of life.

In addition, for many there is the experience of being grandparents, with all the joys this can bring. Once again, relationships need to change to meet the demands of these different roles in the family.

Single People

Single people are often made to feel that they have no status in modern society, and that their contribution is not fully appreciated. Even the church, possibly because of its emphasis on marriage and the family, does not always seem to give much regard to the vocation of the single person. But clearly, God calls some people – both men and women – to choose the vocation of the single life. Others, for many different reasons, remain unmarried. Either way, it can be a life full of potential and commitment.

Many single people make an enormous contribution to the community. Their love goes out to others and is expressed by devoting time and energy to all kinds of activities. Some become the mainstay of elderly parents, or give support to members of their family in need. As a result of the increasing breakdown of marriages, there are many people who now find themselves alone or as single parents. The community needs to be aware that single people can be lonely and socially isolated, and that those who give so much of themselves to others will sometimes need support and appreciation.

Friendship

Another expression of love is the relationship with friends. Friendship with our own or with the opposite sex can be enriching and rewarding. Friendship is a means by which both friends affirm each other and bring affection and support to a relationship. This is valuable because it is freely given and not dependent on duty or obligation.

Family Meals and Hospitality

A meal is a social event. To share food is to share life. A family meal can symbolise, even in the most hidden and obscure way, the bond of affection and willingness to accept one another.

In many religions and cultures, meals and hospitality are seen as profoundly important. There are many accounts of meals in the Gospels: with apostles, with friends, with sinners, celebrating the Passover. Sometimes Jesus was the host, and sometimes the guest.

Hospitality towards others is about relationships, and is a valuable way of showing respect and affection for friends and relatives.

When we are guests of others, we feel warmth and gratitude for what we have received. In giving hospitality, we are expressing a spirituality of openness and generosity.

Personal Reflection

1   What is my network of relationships within my family, and among my friends and colleagues? How do they involve me in giving and receiving?

2   Are there relationships in my life which are difficult and painful? Could I do more towards healing these relationships?

3   Meals often provide a place for building these relationships, and for expressing a willingness to accept one another. What part do they play in my life?

4   What significance, in my life, do I place on cooking, preparing meals, arranging parties and celebrations, inviting people to meals, offering hospitality?

5   In what other ways can I show my appreciation of friends and relatives, if my situation does not allow opportunities for hospitality?

(You may find that this meeting raises a lot of relationship problems. Encourage people to listen to one another and to be supportive; but try to avoid getting involved in giving advice!)

Prayer-Time

Preparation: During this liturgy, we suggest that some 'symbolic food' is shared. This should be very simple; for example: bread, large scone or biscuit, grapes or cherries, or a carafe of wine. Before starting, place the food or drink on a table with a candle.

Introduction: Lord, may your Spirit be with us as we come together to pray in love and unity.

Reading: From the Revelations of Julian of Norwich. in which she tells us that God is Love, and that each of us is loved in a way which we can never fully imagine.

> I saw for certain
> that before ever he made us,
> God loved us;
> and that his love
> has never slackened,
> nor ever shall.
> In this love,
> all his works have been done,
> and in this love
> he has made everything serve us.
> And in this love
> our life is everlasting.
> Our beginning
> was when we were made,
> but the love in which he made us
> has never had beginning.

Reading: In 'To be a Pilgrim', Cardinal Hume tells us how we must love others as God loves us:

> I am thinking of the commandment to love God in response to the love which has first been lavished on us. We must understand clearly what is meant. We so often distort the concept of love. We caricature its reality, we deface it; we think of it as weak, rather insipid, emotional. But the love of which our Lord speaks is demanding. It is a giving experience, selfless and generous. Love wants to give, as much as it wants to receive, and

its model and prototype is the love that is in God.

All: Psalm 102

> My soul, give thanks to the Lord,
> all my being, bless his holy name.
> My soul, give thanks to the Lord
> and never forget all his blessings.
>
> It is he who forgives all your guilt,
> Who heals every one of your ills,
> who redeems your life from the grave,
> who crowns you with love and compassion,
> who fills your life with good things,
> renewing your youth like an eagle's.
>
> Give thanks to the Lord, all his hosts,
> his servants who do his will.
> Give thanks to the Lord, all his works,
> in every place where he rules.
> My soul, give thanks to the Lord.

Hymn: (See suggestions at back)

We have been thinking about hospitality and meals. In giving hospitality, we are reflecting God's bountiful generosity to us, which is often symbolised by food and drink.

Readings: Isaiah 25, 6-8; 55, 1-2

> On this mountain,
> the Lord will prepare for all peoples
> a banquet of rich food,
> a banquet of fine wines,
> a food rich and juicy,
> of fine strained wines.
>
> Oh, come to the water,
> all you who are thirsty;
> though you have no money, come!
> Buy corn without money, and eat;
> and at no cost, wine and milk.

Let us pass round the bread (or....) which we are going to share. In sharing this food, we are expressing symbolically our love and unity. We are also reminded of the Eucharistic meal when, in the breaking of bread, Christ becomes present with us; and which reflects, too, the heavenly agape when all people will be united with God in the everlasting banquet in paradise.

When we have all received a piece of bread, before eating we will say this simple grace together:

Grace: Giver of every good and perfect gift, bless thy people here and everywhere, in their receiving, their giving and their sharing. Through Christ our Lord. Amen

During the sharing, a suitable hymn could be sung, eg the Taize 'Ubi Caritas et Amor'.

Final Prayer: Let us end by saying together Julian of Norwich's prayer:

God feels great delight
to be our Father,
and God feels great delight
to be our Mother,
and God feels great delight
to be our Spouse
and our soul the loved Wife.

Christ feels great delight
that He is our Brother,
and Jesus feels great delight
that he is our Liberator.
These are five great joys
that God wants us to enjoy.
                        Amen

PRAYER

Lay spirituality is concerned with the integration of prayer into the whole of human activity, and is to be lived out in the context of everyday occupations. However, it is also true to say that we need to set aside time for personal prayer, if we are to be aware of God and open to his Spirit in our lives.

Opportunities for Prayer

Setting aside a period each day, however brief, to be with God in silence and attention, is essential to our spiritual growth. For some people, finding this time is not a problem. It is a question of fixing a period in the day and being disciplined enough to keep to it. For others, finding a quiet space in the day may seem almost an impossibility: with pressure of work, lack of privacy, a household of noisy children, shared accommodation, or whatever it may be. In such cases, some ingenuity may be needed to find moments for solitude, such as: driving to work, travelling on the bus or train, taking the dog for a walk, wandering round the garden, preparing the vegetables. We need to look for occasions which bring opportunities for quiet reflection and prayer.

Space

It is necessary, for every person's health and well-being, to find some space in order to relax and be oneself. Being free from the pressure of having to do something is a life enhancing experience in itself. It gives us a chance to catch up on ourselves, and brings us a renewal of spirit.

There is a tendency when we do have a little time to ourselves, to fill it with noise and more activities. Many people find it difficult to cope with being alone and being silent. But it is worthwhile persevering in order to let our minds free-wheel and to simply relax all tension. This may not be prayer as such, but it is certainly an essential preparation for prayer: by allowing oneself to become silent and open so that God can speak to our heart.

Symbols

Symbols are often a means of leading us to prayer. These may take many forms. For example, we know that Christians in Russia set great store in having an icon in their homes to remind themselves of God's presence, and to provide a place where the family can come to pray. Similarly, many people have crucifixes and statues in their homes with the same purpose in mind.

We can also discover, for ourselves, symbolic objects and places which can lead us to prayer. For example, you may create a 'prayer sanctuary' in your house: the spare room, perhaps. Have a special prayer mat, meditation stool, a candle or lamp which you can light to create the right atmosphere. Find objects which inspire you: a work of art, a piece of music etc.

You may find your own symbolic places in your garden or local park: a favourite tree, a place of natural beauty, or anywhere easily accessible where you can be undisturbed and alone, and where you find yourself open to prayer and inner silence.

WAYS INTO PRAYER

Some people seem to have a natural capacity for

prayer, and are blessed by a special gift from God. But most of us have more of a struggle, and need to search for different approaches to prayer, to find one which suits us best. How we pray is very personal, and often depends on our personality and temperament. There is no **one**, approved way to God. Neither does God judge us by our apparent success or failure. We are told in the Scriptures that, when we do not know how to pray, the Spirit prays within us, on our behalf.

Using the Body

Finding a way to relax and to centre oneself can be a great help in preparing for prayer. Yoga and T'ai Chi are both Eastern disciplines which use the body to create a sense of harmony and inner peace. Meditation uses breathing and posture as a way of achieving inner silence.

Some people find that making gestures of the body, such as using their hands, kneeling, bowing, can be helpful ways of cutting through the distractions and tensions which come upon them when they turn to prayer.

Feelings

In the past, we have often been told that prayer is an exercise of the mind and the will, and that our emotions have to be firmly put on one side. Certainly, prayer is not simply indulging in mulling over our immediate reactions to people and situations! However, we come to God as we are, and feelings are part of ourselves. And there are certain times when we may have particular worries and concerns, or perhaps we are devastated by some event in our lives or in the world, when it is quite impossible to put feelings away. Then, our feelings become our prayer, and we put before God the impact which these events are having upon us, and we freely acknowledge our reactions. After all, the psalmists were very free in expressing their anger, resentment, anxiety, joy and thanksgiving.

Spiritual Books

Reading Scripture and religious books can also be a good background to prayer. Pondering and reflecting on the Scriptures disposes us towards God when we come to pray. Reading about prayer or theology widens our knowledge and understanding. Contemporary spiritual writers encourage us and help us to persevere by sharing their own prayer experiences. In his book entitled 'Prayer', Abishiktananda says:-

> The life of prayer, the life of contemplation, is simply to realise God's Presence to us. It is, therefore, not a special way of life reserved for those individuals who are called to get away from the world and to dwell in the desert. Contemplation and prayer ought to be the very breath of every disciple of Christ.

Personal Reflection

1   Do I find opportunities for prayer in my life? How do I pray? What helps me most to become prayerful?

2   How balanced is my life? Do I find space for myself when I can be silent and alone?

3   What are the things which hinder me from praying or from reading the Scriptures or other spiritual books?

4   Do I find it helpful to pray with others in groups or in the parish? What sort of liturgies do I find feed my own prayer life?

The primary VOCATION OF THE LAITY IS TO BECOME HOLY PEOPLE.

Prayer-Time

There is no Prayer-Time prepared for this meeting, as it seems more appropriate to allow the group to spend some time in personal prayer.

Preparation: It is important to create a peaceful and prayerful atmosphere. Depending on where you are meeting, it could be helpful to arrange the chairs in a circle, with some focal point such as a bowl of flowers, candles etc. and, if possible, lowered lighting. If you are going to use some background music, have this ready, also.

When everyone is gathered, the leader could ask each person to adopt the posture which they find most helpful: sitting, kneeling, sitting on the floor, etc., but remind them of the importance of using the body in prayer. It is suggested that they close their eyes.

Music is very helpful for creating an atmosphere at the start of the session, but choose something which is not too familiar. Tapes of peaceful meditation music are available. The music could also be played at the end of the period of prayer, to indicate that the meditation is drawing to a close, and to provide a period when people can return to everyday life. Each group must decide on the length of this prayer time: possibly 15-20 minutes might be suitable for most groups.

Some groups may like to try a relaxation exercise to lead into the meditation. It is also a way of introducing a method of quietening oneself and letting go of tensions.

Relaxation Exercises

Sit comfortably, but in an upright position, with your feet resting flat on the ground. Shut your eyes. Let your hands rest quietly, in an open way.

Now, try consciously to relax your body, starting with your feet. Let them really rest on the ground.

Now, go upwards through your body: Be aware of your ankles, your calves, your thighs. Let all tensions go .... (pause).

Let your attention now go to your stomach. Relax. Let all tensions go .... (pause).

Be aware of your buttocks and your back; the feel of your body resting in the chair. Let the chair take your weight; feel your body rest on the chair; feel your clothes .... (pause).

Now, be conscious of your shoulders. Hunch them up, and let them go. Relax your arms and your hands. Let all tensions go.... (pause).

Give your attention, now, to your neck and face. Relax your facial muscles and your forehead. Smooth out all tensions...(pause).

If you have pain in any part of your body, be aware of it. Accept it, and give it your attention .... (pause).

Now, concentrate on your breathing. Follow your breath. Be aware of your incoming breath, and follow your breath as it leaves your body. Draw in ... breathe out ... find your own quiet rhythm.

(Suggestions for 'Ways into Prayer' are given on pages 108-109. You may feel it appropriate to talk about these as part of the meeting.)

After the meditation, allow time for people to come out of it quite slowly, before you close the meeting. If you wish, you could end with the following prayer:

Final Prayer:

>The Lord bless us and keep us.
>
>The Lord let his face shine upon us and be gracious to us.
>
>The Lord look upon us kindly, and give us peace.
>
> Amen

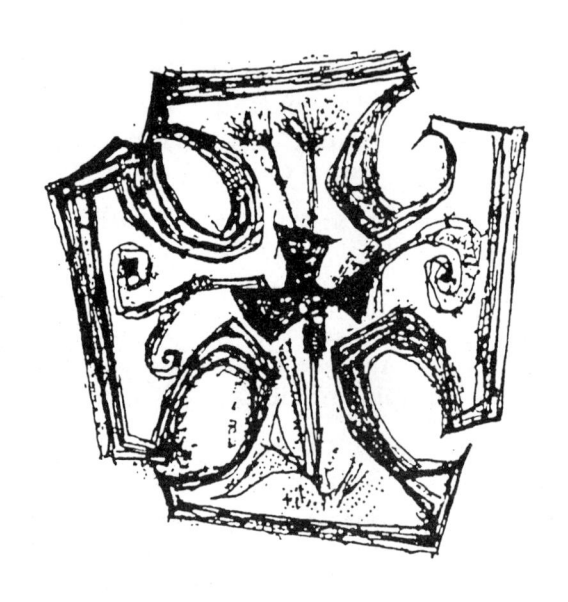

IN THE DARKNESS

In these sessions, we have emphasised the positive view of humanity and of the world. We have stressed the basic goodness of the human person and the wonder and value of the whole of creation. However, we all know from our own experience that the world is only in the process of being redeemed; each individual, and society as a whole, needs transforming and renewing. This affects us in many different ways.

Secular Values

In spite of the fact that many of our institutions in Britain are basically Christian in origin, we now live in an almost totally secular society.

Many individuals continue to demonstrate strong commitment to others, and to live highly moral lives; but generally speaking, as a nation we live by secular standards. These may be humanitarian in outlook, and express care for the individual and the good of the community; but nevertheless, our society seems to be increasingly losing its way, putting emphasis on wrong things. We see around us great stress on the material: consumerism, dishonesty, unethical practices in business, exploitation, increasing violence in every direction.

There are also many signs of lack of concern for others, as shown by racial disharmony, prejudice of many kinds, homelessness, poverty, etc. As members of this society, we all share to some extent in the guilt for these communal sins, and have to accept our share of responsibility.

Disasters and Wars

At an international level, there are constant tensions and situations of conflict between nations, and many human tragedies and disasters. Our modern media puts us in touch in a graphic way with these events, so that we can hardly fail to share the sufferings of the people concerned. In the midst of all these disasters and conflicts, we must endeavour to have faith and trust in God. As Christians, we are 'people of hope', knowing that - whatever terrible state we seem to be in at times - we believe God is alive and present in our world; that, in every tragedy, God is present, however distressing the circumstances.

Personal Sinfulness

As well as all the disorders in the world, we also have to acknowledge our personal weakness and sinfulness; our inability to cope with our own inner darkness, with the feelings and movements within us about which we are ashamed. This aspect of ourselves is frightening, and we try to avoid it. We find all sorts of ways of escaping from our inner turmoil. Facing this darkness, admitting our faults is never easy. But our spiritual journey leads us towards accepting our inadequacies, our real despair and regrets. It is in facing this personal pain that we can become channels of Christ's redeeming and healing grace.

Suffering

Suffering comes to us all, in one way or another. Also, we constantly meet people who are suffering, often through no fault of their own: through sickness, accidents, handicap, rejection and loss of all kinds. Hurts, rejections and disappointments can accompany people through life, causing immense suffering. Death brings its own pain, whether it is the death of a loved one, or the fear and anxiety about our own death.

As Christians, we share in this pain and suffering, and find it no easier to bear than other people. But our faith in Jesus Christ, who suffered in his life and finally in his death, teaches us that suffering is part of our human condition. In some way, it is through embracing this suffering that we are able to make it fruitful. Unless the grain of wheat dies, it does not bring forth the shoot.

So it is in suffering and dying with Christ that we are able to release to the world the energy and life of the resurrection.

Reconciliation

There is great need in the world for reconciliation and forgiveness, in order to heal past wounds and broken relationships. This is true whether between individuals, families or nations. An outstanding Christian virtue is the willingness and ability to show forgiveness to those who have hurt or injured us. When Jesus was asked by one of his disciples 'How often should we forgive? Seven times?' Jesus answered: 'No! Seventy times seven!'

The sacrament of reconciliation is one means by which we, as individuals can be strengthened through God's grace; where we can face our own personal sinfulness, and so be reconciled to the community.

We ourselves can also become enablers of reconciliation: by bringing people together, by learning skills of communication, by allowing people to air their grievances, and by listening to "the other side's" point of view. All these are ways of healing wounds and bringing about forgiveness. All these are ways of healing divisions and bringing new light into those dark areas of discord and disharmony.

Personal Reflection

1. What are the dark areas in my life which I find most difficult? How do I cope with my fears and anxieties: In my personal life? In my prayer?

2. How can I take on board the things which cause me hurt and pain, without becoming bitter and angry?

3. What are the dark areas in our society which cause me most concern?
   Am I able to witness to my faith and my trust in God by a positive attitude and a hopeful outlook?

4. Are there times when I feel a sense of failure and utter powerlessness in the face of the weight of suffering of those around me? How can I become open to the Spirit within me, so that I am able to be a channel of life-enhancing strength to others?

5. Belief in God does not necessarily take away our fear and suffering, but if we feel precious in God's eyes we are able to accept it and move on. Am I open to God's unconditional love of me?

Prayer-Time

Preparation: It would be appropriate to have either a small candle for each person, or one large candle, which can be lighted during this liturgy.

Introduction: O God, our heavenly Father, we ask you to send your Spirit to be with us. Help us to be open, so that we may grow in love and knowledge of you. Give us courage to face the

Consider the church as the people of God, a great river flowing through history, watering the garden of the world with the mercy of God things we must change in our lives.

Reading: John 15 vv 5, 2.

> I am the vine, you are the branches.
> Those who abide in me, and I in them,
> they are the ones that bear much fruit,
> from me you can do nothing.
> Every branch that does bear fruit
> my Father prunes,
> that it may bear still more fruit.

We know that the gardener has to prune the trees from time to time, in order to strengthen the tree or make it bear more flowers or fruit. The good gardener knows exactly how and when to cut back.

All: Psalm 26 - a psalm of trust and confidence in God's care.

> The Lord is my light and my help;
> whom shall I fear?
> The Lord is the stronghold of my life;
> before whom shall I shrink?
>
> There is one thing I ask of the Lord,
> for this I long:
> to live in the house of the Lord
> all the days of my life;
> to savour the sweetness of the Lord,
> to behold his temple.
>
> For there he keeps me safe in his tent
> in the day of evil.
> He hides me in the shelter of his tent;
> on a rock he sets me safe.

Readings: Two extracts from 'This is the Laity' paras 54 and 38:

> Within a society that has lost
> a sense of human suffering,
> the Church has to make the news resound
> that suffering can have a positive meaning

for the individual person
and, indeed, for society as well.
This is because each person
is called to share
in Christ's redemptive suffering
and the joy of resurrection.

Silent reflection

One aspect of the Church's mission
is to accept every human being,
especially the sick and the weak,
with love and generosity.
The Church sees all life
as a gift from God.
In the darkness of today's world
of pessimism and selfishness
the Church stands for life;
in the face of the world's 'No'
it gives a living 'Yes'.

Pause, to think about how we can show that we say 'Yes' to life, both personally and in our attitude to every day.

Light the candle(s) here.

Prayer: Adapted from the Experimental Liturgy Book.

Let us say this prayer together, to ask God to give us the courage to say 'Yes':

Lord, you have chosen us,
and given us the wonder of human life.
You have loved us forever,
and shared with us your divine life.
And yet, we know we fail in many ways.
We acknowledge our sin,
our sickening selfishness,
our refusal to love and to give.
We beg you, now, as we come before you,
to forgive us,
to give us new life,

> to free us from all in our lives
> that is less than Christian.
> We beg forgiveness
> from all our brothers and sisters
> whom we have used,
> whom we have ignored,
> with whom we have not shared our love.
> Lord God,
> restore us to life,
> make us new,
> make all things new,
> through Jesus Christ,
> your Son, our Lord.   Amen

In his book 'Original Blessing', Matthew Fox says this:

> Facing the darkness, admitting the pain, allowing pain to be pain, is never easy. This is why courage is the most essential virtue on the spiritual journey. But if we fail to let pain be pain - then pain will haunt us in nightmarish ways. We will become pain's victims, instead of the healers we might become.

Recite Together:

Lord, give us this courage we need to follow our path of life. We cannot escape suffering in our lives, and some of us have more than others. May we accept what comes our way, with trust in your constant and loving goodness, and the belief that, as Julian of Norwich says: 'All will be well, and all manner of things will be well.' We ask this in Jesus' name. Amen

Finish with a suitable hymn of trust and hope.

CREATION SPIRITUALITY

We read in Genesis how God created the heavens and the earth. Then, having created man and woman, God instructed them to 'fill the earth and subdue it and have dominion over the fish of the sea and over the birds of the air and every living thing that moves upon the earth and all the seeds and trees'. There can be few precepts in the Bible which humanity has taken so much to heart. The 'dominion' which the human race was given over the universe has in many ways proved to be thoughtless and destructive, rather than responsible and caring.

We are only now beginning to see how we have misused and vandalised the earth we have been given to care for. In Genesis, there is another creation story: 'And the Lord God planted a garden in Eden, in the east; and there he put the man he had formed... The Lord God took the man and put him in the garden of Eden to till it and keep it.' This account puts more emphasis on God creating human beings to share in the garden, to enjoy it, preserve and cultivate it.

Early Church

The early church appears to have been aware of this close inter-relationship between humanity and the whole of creation. Paul writes to the Colossians that 'Christ is the image of the invisible God, the first-born of all creation; for in him all things were created, in heaven and on earth.' Paul stresses that Christ has not only redeemed the human race but the whole of creation which 'has been groaning in travail together until now' and he says: 'We know that the whole of creation itself will be set free from the bondage to decay and obtain the glorious liberty of the children of God.'

Over the years, the church's teaching has not been outstandingly 'environmental' as we know it today. But, through the centuries, there have been many prophetic voices bringing to awareness our close link with creation: Benedict, who saw that spirituality included care for the earth, and whose monks tended and farmed their monastic land to such good effect; Francis, who recognised his personal dependence on the planet, and praised and honoured God through Brother Sun and Sister Moon; from Julian of Norwich in the 14th century: 'It seemed to me that God is everything that is good and the goodness of everything is God', to Teilhard de Chardin in the 20th century with his cosmic spirituality.

The Environment

Most people find it easy to be close to God when surrounded by the beauty of nature. In fact, for those of us who live in congested urban cities, it is a vital need for us to get out into the open countryside, or to places where we are in touch with growing things. To preserve our sanity, and for the sake of the human spirit, it is essential that we conserve and protect our natural environment.

Wherever we live, we can attempt to improve our surroundings and make them more beautiful, whether it is in our homes, gardens, or local communities. These are all ways of showing respect and reverence for living things whether human, plants, animals, birds, insects, etc. In caring for them, we are expressing our appreciation and thanksgiving for creation.

Ecology

Today, we know that the whole world is in deep trouble with regard to the environment. It is only recently that the human race has come to realise the effects of industrial pollution, the abuse of natural resources, the results of artificial fertilisers and insecticides, and all the other aspects of global distress. Every day we hear more stories of environmental tragedies, often the consequence of greed, mismanagement, lack of thought about future generations. It is going to need the combined skill and cooperation of men and women throughout the world if we are to conserve our planet.

This is a basically religious issue in which Christians must be involved, to ensure that justice is done to preserve the earth and living things, and that all creatures have a right to life. As the Synod document states in para 43:

> Humanity has the God-given task
> of 'cultivating the garden' of our planet ...
> When it comes to the natural world
> we are subject,
> not only to biological laws,
> but to moral laws as well.

Thoughtful Gestures

We know that bringing about change and working for a more just society with regard to the preservation of the earth is an extremely technical and complicated business and has to be tackled on a world-wide scale. We may feel that it is very difficult for an individual person to make much headway or bring about any truly radical change. But lay spirituality surely includes each of us making some thoughtful gesture towards improving our environment and conserving its resources. This could involve such things as: taking bottles and newspapers to the re-cycling depot; joining local pressure groups about your community environment; or even writing to your Member of Parliament about issues of concern. International campaigns – about the rain forest or saving the whale – not only have their effect, but they also serve to remind us of the world issues.

Personal Reflection

1 Do I find time in my life to be in touch with growing and living things? How important is this in my normal routine?

2 Does my home reflect my concern for the environment? Are there ways in which I could try to be creative and improve my immediate environment and bring about more beauty and harmony?

3 To what extent can I involve myself in efforts towards preserving the environment and conserving resources in my local neighbourhood?

4 Could I do more to keep myself informed of conservation and ecological issues? Am I involved in local or national pressure groups?

Prayer-Time

Preparation: A focal point for this liturgy could be plants, flowers, fruit, etc; or, if you prefer, some dishes of dried grain, dried fruit, rice, a jug of water. You may find some suitable poster as a background.

Introduction: O God, we would thank you for all the bright things of life. Help us to see them, and to count them, and to remember them, that our lives may flow in ceaseless praise for

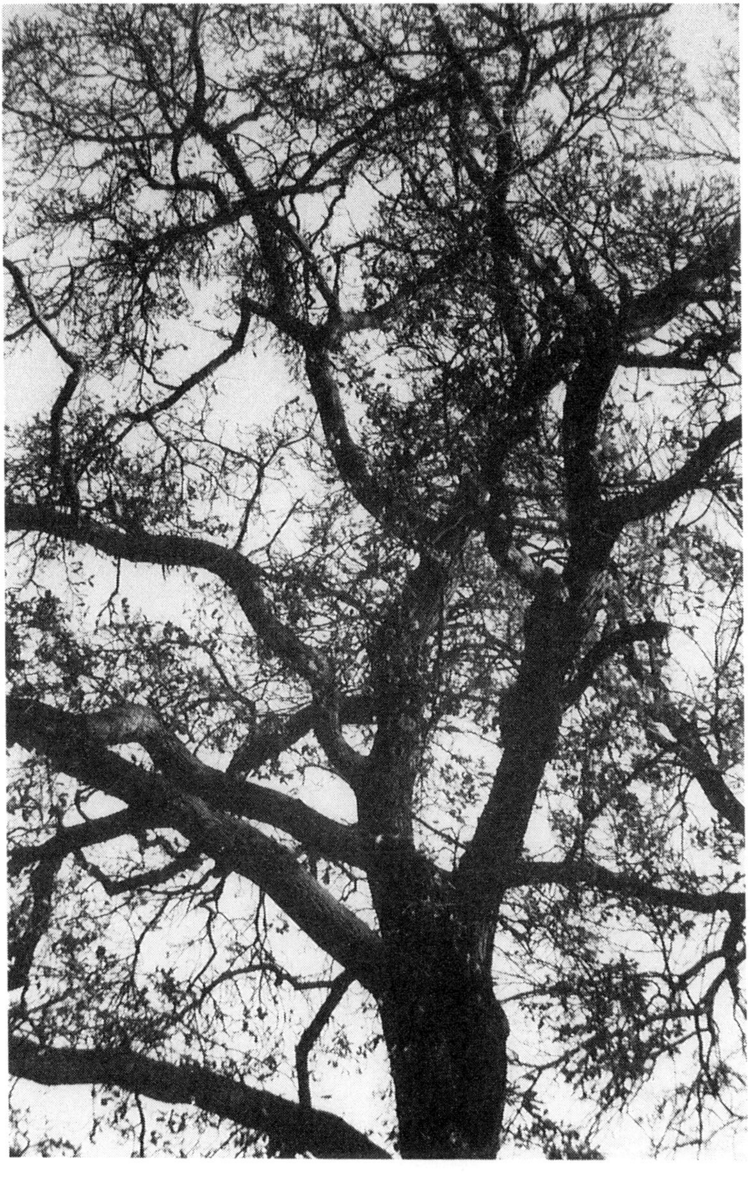

the sake of Jesus Christ our Lord.

Reading: Extract from the Address of the Red Indian Chief Seattle to the President of the United States who was buying his people's land:

> Will you teach your children what we have taught our children: that the earth is our Mother? What befalls the earth, befalls all the children of the earth. This we know: The earth does not belong to us; we belong to the earth. All things are connected, like the blood that unites us all. We do not weave the web of life; we are merely strands in it. Whatever we do to the web, we do to ourselves. We love the earth as a new-born loves its mother's heartbeat. We ask you to love it as we have loved it; care for it as we have cared for it... Preserve the land for all children, and love it as God loves us all.

All: Psalm 64

> To you our praise is due
> in Sion, O God.
> To you we pay our vows,
> you who hear our prayer.

> The ends of the earth stand in awe
> at the sight of your wonders.
> The lands of sunrise and sunset
> you fill with your joy.

> You care for the earth, give it water,
> you fill it with riches.
> Your river in heaven brims over
> to provide its grain.

> And thus you provide for the earth.
> You drench its furrows,
> you level it, soften it with showers,
> you bless its growth.

Reading: from 'This is the Laity' para 43:

> God's words 'to dominate' the creation
> give humanity no freedom to abuse it.
> When it comes to the natural world
> we are subject,
> not only to biological laws,
> but to moral laws as well.
> And they cannot be violated
> without disastrous consequences.
> A true concept of development
> cannot ignore the way the planet is used,
> nor which of its resources are renewable,
> nor the consequences
> of haphazard industrialisation.
> These considerations make us realise
> that there is a moral dimension
> to development.

Recite Together: The Canticle of the Sun

> O most high, almighty, good Lord God,
> to thee belong praise, glory, honour and blessing.
>
> Praise be my Lord God with all his creatures,
> and especially our brother the sun,
> who brings us the day
> and who brings us the light;
> fair is he and shines with a very great splendour.
> O Lord, he signifies to us thee.
>
> Praised be my Lord for our sister the moon,
> and for the stars,
> the which he has set clear and lovely in heaven.
>
> Praised be my Lord for our brother the wind,
> and for air and cloud, calms and all weather,
> by which thou upholdest life in all creatures.
>
> Praised be my Lord for our sister water,
> who is very serviceable unto us
> and humble and precious and clean.
>
> Praised be my Lord for our brother fire,
> through whom thou givest us

light in the darkness;
and he is bright and pleasant
and mighty and strong.

Praised be my Lord for our mother the earth,
the which doth sustain us and keep us,
and bringeth forth divers fruits,
and flowers of many colours, and grass.

Praise ye and bless ye the Lord,
and give thanks unto him,
and serve him with great humility. Amen

Here, Francis tells us we must 'serve God with humility'. We need to approach this tremendous task of bringing balance and harmony to our planet with humility and respect. This means being at peace with one another as well as ensuring justice and freedom to all living things. Could we make this covenant together today, to do just that.

Recite Together:

We covenant today with one another:

- with every living creature and all on which we depend;
- with all that is on earth and with the earth itself;
- with all that lives in the waters and with the waters themselves;
- with all creatures of the air, and with the air itself;
- with all that is warm with life, and with the living fire.

We commit ourselves today to put away all selfishness and greed, and to embrace one another and all creation in joy and peace.

Final Prayer:

May he that provided the seed for the sowing, the hand for doing, the mind for thinking, and the heart for loving, the Father, Son and Holy Spirit, bless us and preserve us all the days of our life. Amen

From the writings of Julian of Norwich:

> There is a treasure in the earth
> that is a food tasty and pleasing
> to the Lord.
>
> Be a gardener.
> Dig and ditch,
> toil and sweat,
> and turn the earth upside down
> and seek the dampness
> and water the plants in time.
> Continue this labour
> and make sweet floods to run
> and noble and abundant fruits
> to spring.
> Take this food and drink
> and carry it to God
> as your true worship.

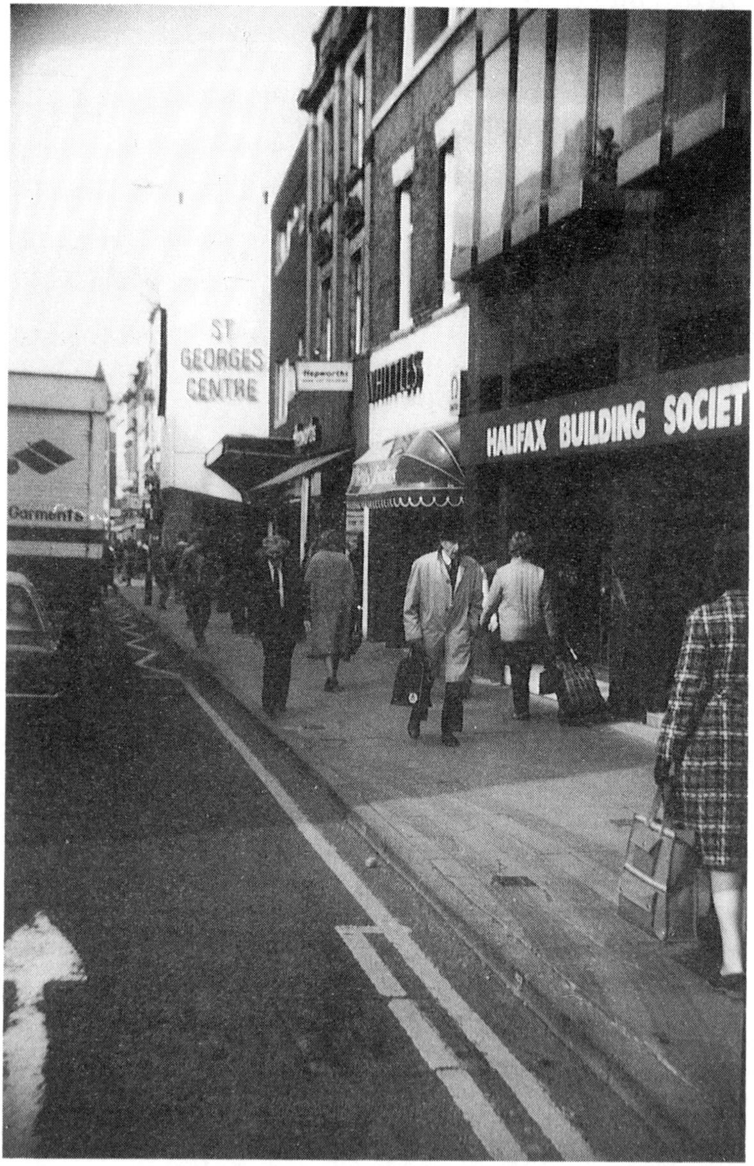
ST GEORGES CENTRE
HALIFAX BUILDING SOCIET
Garments

OUR JOURNEY

We each have our own journey to travel and our own response to the events and circumstances of our lives. With the help of the Spirit, we act and respond to God in our own characteristic way, and through our own gifts and insights.

First, we need to recognise our own human dignity, and live in a manner which gives respect to ourselves as a unique person. God is present to us at all times, and his plans for us unfold as life goes on.

Looking back over our lives, we may reflect on the events which have happened to us - both joyful and sad, the people who have influenced us, the situations which have brought about change, or given us new direction.

Discerning God's Way

From time to time, we have to make important decisions about our lives. This is not just a question of deciding what is the best thing to do, but also the path God wants us to follow.

It may be a choice of vocation or career, choosing a marriage partner, changing course in one way or another. Discovering God's will for us means praying hard for guidance, listening to the Spirit in our hearts, listening to what others say, discerning the gifts we have been given, and considering our own situation. Should these decisions involve others, then we have to be sure that our decision does not limit their freedom and growth.

It may be that what we know to be the right

course of action is very hard for us to follow. It is not good enough to **know** what God wants; we have to **do** what God wants. But we have the assurance that God's grace will give us the capacity to act. Leo the Great said: 'The One who confers the dignity will give the strength.'

God wants us to grow into mature men and women. As we go through life, we have to take responsibility for our own actions and decisions, learning to trust ourselves and God's life within us, and have confidence in our own wisdom and judgment.

Painful Memories

Of course, we are going to make mistakes and take wrong turnings. We are going to experience bad patches as life unfolds. Things will happen which may bring suffering and heartache. Events from the past could have deeply wounded us and may continue to arouse strong feelings. Perhaps we still feel anger and resentment, and may have difficulty in forgiving. Or it could be the future which fills us with anxiety and depression.

These negative feelings are not easy to bear, and often make us feel guilty and unworthy of God's love and care. But we can be assured that God understands the human heart and is with us in our sufferings. Feelings are real, and it is right to acknowledge them; they are part of being human. At the same time, we need to find ways of freeing ourselves from these spirals of self-pity or depression. Otherwise, they can cripple us and prevent us from becoming the person we are meant to be.

If we are at fault, and aware of our sinfulness, we can find forgiveness through the sacrament of reconciliation. In other situations, perhaps counselling could help us to face up to unresolved problems in the past, or anxieties about the future. Having the courage to sort out some long-standing relationship difficulty may also bring peace, and a chance to start again. But where no effort on our part can change the situation, then we must put this pain before God, and ask for his strength and grace to help us accept these feelings and heal us. In the Old Testament, we learn that Job was not given any relief from his sufferings, but he did find God through them.

Guidance

Baptism makes us members of the Church and, through her ministry of teaching and sanctifying, we are helped along our personal journey.

The Bishops and their priests, as ministers of the Word, serve the Church by preaching and teaching the Good News. They help us to grow in faith, and relate it to everyday life and to the issues of the day.

The Church can be described as a sacrament: a sign and a means of union with God, and a sign of the unity of all human beings. The worship and sacraments of the Church help to renew our life in Christ, and bring about communion with other people.

The teaching of Jesus in the Gospels, and the Church's social and moral teaching, help to form our consciences to enable us to discern what is right and wrong. But ultimately, a person's own conscience is the guide as to how he or she should behave and act.

It can be very supportive for lay people to come together regularly, to share their experience of living as Christians and in praying together. In this way, they are able to help one another in relation to family life, work, prayer, etc. It is important, also, to grow in faith and understanding by means of the Scriptures and keeping ourselves up-to-date with spiritual and pastoral issues.

Grateful Hearts

We recognise God's love and care for us by expressing our thanks and praise for our many blessings; by cultivating a grateful heart which appreciates the good things in our lives; by being thankful for our very being, and the world in which we live; by being positive in our outlook, not just in mindless optimism but in a belief that God has won the victory. So much of our energy is spent in going over the past, or worrying about the future, that we fail to live in the present!

Personal Reflection

1. Who are the people who have been a positive influence to me in my life? How have they helped me to grow and develop?
2. Have I any memories of the past which continue to burden me because they have not been resolved; or because I am left with feelings which hinder my freedom, prayer life, and peace of mind?
3. What are the things which help me, in my present life, to move forward; and what are the things which hold me back?
4. In what ways do I increase in knowledge of my faith, and learn about the issues being discussed in the Church?

Prayer-Time

Preparation: There is no particular symbol or preparation required for this liturgy, other than arranging the room to create a prayerful and peaceful atmosphere. In an ongoing group, each person could have been asked to bring to this meeting a photograph taken of themselves at some period in their lives. These photographs could be displayed during the liturgy.

Introduction: Lord, we come together to thank you for all you have given us, for watching over us throughout our lives, and for being a light to guide us on our way.

Reading: from Hildegard of Bingen

> God has created me
> God is my Lord,
> having dominion over me.

> God is also my strength
> for I can wish to do
> nothing good without God.

> Through God I have living spirit.
> Through God I have life and movement.
> Through God I learn, I find my path.

> If I call in truth,
> this God and Lord directs my steps,
> setting my feet
> to the rhythm of his precepts.

> I run like a deer that seeks its spring.

Recite Together: Psalm 15

> Preserve me, God, I take refuge in you.
> I say to the Lord: 'You are my God.
> My happiness lies in you alone.'

> O Lord,
> it is you who are my portion and cup;
> it is you yourself who are my prize.
> The lot marked out for me is my delight:
> welcome indeed the heritage that falls to me!

> I will bless the Lord who gives me counsel,
> who even at night directs my heart.

> I keep the Lord ever in my sight:
> since he is at my right hand,
> I shall stand firm.
>
> You will show me the path of life,
> the fullness of joy in your presence,
> at your right hand happiness for ever.

Reading: from 'This is the Laity' para 58

> God has loved us from eternity
> as unique individuals,
> but it is only as our lives unfold
> that his plans for us are revealed.
> This is something that happens day by day.
>
> To grow in the knowledge
> of all that our faith gives us,
> to live it out more fully –
> this is the task awaiting all Christians
> at every moment of their lives.

•

Let us now be silent for a short time, while we think of all the people who have helped us during life's journey:

- those who have loved us;
- those who have been a special influence;
- those who have guided and supported us at critical times;
- and those on whom we now rely to be our companions.

Silent Reflection

In thanksgiving for all these blessings, let us recite together a verse from Psalm 102:

> My soul, give thanks to the Lord,
> all my being, bless his holy name.
> My soul, give thanks to the Lord
> and never forget all his blessings.

Reading: from Ezekiel 36, 26-27, in which we ask God to renew our hearts and make us more full of love and compassion.

A new heart I will give you, and a new spirit I will put within you; and I will take out of your flesh the heart of stone and give you a heart of flesh. And I will put my spirit within you, and cause you to walk in my statutes and be careful to observe my ordinances.

Final Prayer: Attributed to St. Patrick

May the strength of God
guide me this day,
and may his power preserve me.

May the wisdom of God instruct me;
the eye of God watch over me;
the ear of God hear me;
the word of God give sweetness to my speech;
the hand of God defend me;
and may I follow the way of God.

WE DO NOT WEAVE THE WEB OF LIFE; WE ARE MERELY STRANDS IN IT.
Chief Seattle

EVANGELISATION

Christ's command to preach the Gospel never loses its force. Today, the present state of the world makes his call even more urgent. He calls each person by name, and we are each called to preach and evangelise in Christ's name.

Personal Call

First, evangelisation begins with the conversion of ourselves to the good news of the Gospel and to the integration of Christ's teaching into our lives. Our faith and belief in God is personal and demands our complete response and commitment above everything else. We can only open the door to Christ for others when he is truly the centre of our own lives.

Bearing Witness

Through baptism, we enter into discipleship and share in Christ's ministry. Christ gives us the same message that he gave to his disciples: 'As the Father has sent me, so I send you'. And he promised that the Holy Spirit would be with us, giving us the strength and power to further the Kingdom.

Healing and Reconciliation

As well as teaching and preaching, Jesus went about healing those who were sick and handicapped. In his day, these were the outcasts of society. By healing them, Jesus was showing that the reign of God had begun, and this was a sign of the Kingdom, within which everyone would be welcome.

As prophesied in Isaiah, 'He has sent me to bring good news to the poor, to bind up hearts that are broken, to proclaim liberty to captives, freedom to those in prison.'

So, one way we can evangelise is by sharing in Christ's healing ministry, and we can do this in our own way, within our own situation. The 'poor' and the 'lame', the 'sick' and 'suffering' are all around us.

Perhaps our talent lies in direct healing, in listening and counselling, in bringing about changes in our neighbourhood to benefit the poor. Perhaps our gifts will lead us to mend discord between individuals or groups, by helping to resolve problems, bringing down barriers between people. All these are ways of setting people 'free' to begin to experience the Kingdom of God.

Transforming Society

Evangelisation means showing society the relevance of the Gospel message to its life and problems. Whilst believing that the world is basically good, at the same time we know it to be in great need of transformation and renewal. Our responsibility is to work for the growth and development of the world, to share in Christ's ongoing redemption of the world, to spread his Kingdom of justice, love and peace.

Consequently, the redemption of the world is brought about through our involvement in action towards social justice, liberation and the building up of our society to benefit the common good. Christians challenge the world in areas of work, family life, politics, business, trade unions, local and central government, and so on.

Proclaiming the Word

We live in a secular society which has largely forgotten or rejected Christian and religious values. There are many issues today - social, political, medical, scientific - which present new challenges to all of us, and about which we need to work out new ethical practice. We must not be slow at joining in the debate and giving the Christian view, to ensure the preservation of human rights and personal dignity.

There may be times when we want to express our Christian belief in a more direct and explicit way, in order to show that Christian teaching has a contribution to make to significant moments in human life, and to human dilemmas. Some of us are able to proclaim the good news through the media, the written word, music, drama, art, etc, using our imagination and creative talent.

Worshipping Community

The whole Church is called to be evangelical, and to announce the good news to the world.

These sessions are deliberately addressed to individuals and concerned with personal spirituality. Nevertheless, as members of the Church, we have a responsibility to share in the local church's communal task of evangelisation, to contribute to the sacramental and liturgical life of the parish, to ensure that it is an outward-looking community concerned with the needs of the local neighbourhood.

Towards Unity

Division between the Christian churches is a source of scandal, and therefore part of living-out the Gospel must include working towards unity, and sharing in joint efforts of bearing witness to Christ.

In addition, as we now live in a multi-racial and multi-faith society, we have to be open to the rich contribution which other faiths and cultures make to our community, and recognise that God's spirit is alive in non-Christian religions.

We need to work with all people of goodwill, whatever their beliefs, including those who claim no belief in God.

Personal Reflection

1. Remembering that evangelisation is, first and foremost, a call to personal conversion and renewal, how do I nourish my inner self so that I am able to proclaim the good news?

2. How do I get in touch with my creativity and imagination, so that I discover ways of telling others about what I believe?

3. We each have our own special gifts and opportunities for evangelisation. In the areas mentioned in this meeting, where do you feel you may be able to exercise a ministry?

Bearing Witness - aiming to witness to the Gospel by the sort of life one leads and in one's care of others.

Healing and Reconciliation - bringing healing and freedom both to individuals and to situations of disharmony or difficulty.

Transforming Society - working for change, in order to bring about a more just and compassionionate society.

Proclaiming the Word - either by direct teaching or preaching or, through various means, telling people of the good news.

Parish Community - helping to build up your local parish community to be a sign of God's love in the neighbourhood.

Christian Unity - working with other Christians and furthering unity.

Prayer-Time

Preparation: The visual aid for this liturgy could be an open Bible on a table, with either a candle or a lamp.

Introduction: Lord God, through Jesus you show the mystery of your love. Through him, you send your Spirit to our world. We ask you to be with us as we seek to bring your Kingdom into this world.

Reading: Mark 9, 2-8

And after six days, Jesus took with him Peter and James and John, and led them up a high mountain apart by themselves; and he was transfigured before them, and his garments became glistening, intensely white, as no fuller on earth could bleach them.

And there appeared to them Elijah with Moses; and they were talking to Jesus. And Peter said to Jesus, 'Master, it is well that we are here; let us make three booths, one for you and one for Moses and one for Elijah.' For he did not know what to say, for they were exceedingly afraid.

And a cloud overshadowed them, and a voice came out of the cloud 'This is my beloved Son, listen to him'. And suddenly, looking around, they no longer saw any one with them but only Jesus.

The three apostles were privileged to see Jesus transfigured and glorified, and this was such a fantastic experience, they wanted to remain with that glory on the mountain; but Jesus told them they must go down from the mountain and witness to this glory to the people.

Today, **we** are asked to witness to Christ in

the same way. We are called to open the door to Christ that he may enter.

Reading: from 'This is the Laity' para 34:

> Pope John Paul urges everyone
> to open the door to Christ,
> to let him enter, with his power,
> within the boundaries of states,
> into all the fields of culture,
> into political and economic systems.
> He urges people not to fear to do this.
> Only Christ knows what is in people.
> Let him speak to their doubts
> and uncertainties.
> He has the words of eternal life.
>
> To open the door to Christ,
> to accept him into humanity itself,
> poses no threat to anyone.
> It is the only path
> on which it is possible to arrive
> at the fullness of truth
> and the dignity of the individual.
>
> The Church owes it to humanity
> to produce the simple, powerful truth
> that God loves every human being,
> that Christ came on earth
> for every one of them
> as **The Way, the Truth and the Life.**

．

Christ will transfigure our weakness and let his light shine through us.

Reading: from Brother Roger of Taize

> As the light of Christ is at work in the heart of our inner nights, so too it is active in the obscurity of the world. In this way, God is taking humanity upon himself, living in the midst of the human family. Christians are bearers of the Spirit of the Risen

Christ; with great discretion, they communicate the presence of God himself.

Recite Together: Prayer by Caryl Micklem

> Lord Jesus Christ,
> you are the light of the world:
> light up our lives when we are in darkness.
>
> In the darkness of our uncertainty
> when we don't know what to do,
> when decisions are hard to take:
> Lord, give light to guide us.
>
> In the darkness of our anxiety
> when we are worried about
> what the future may bring,
> when we don't know where to turn:
> Lord, give us the light of your peace.
>
> In the darkness of our despair
> when life seems empty,
> when we feel there is no point in going on:
> Lord, give us light and your hope.
>
> In your name we ask it.

Silent Prayer

BIDDING PRAYERS: if desired

OUR FATHER

HYMN: (see back for suggestions)

Final Prayer: From the Commitment Ceremony for the inauguration of the Churches Together in England, Southwark Cathedral, August 1990

> As the seed grows secretly in the earth
> as the yeast rises in the dough,
> may the power of God be at work in us.
> May we witness, together with all Christians
> to the glory of God
> and the fulfillment of his Kingdom.

HE is there with us, in us, over & under us, inside and out — a cloud of UNKNOWING, a SHIELD to defend us.

Sheila Cassidy

JUSTICE AND PEACE

> Mercy and Faithfulness have met
> Justice and Peace have embraced

These lines from Psalm 84 give a beautiful and prophetic vision of God's Kingdom. It embodies a world beyond imagining, where mercy and justice will reign, bringing peace to everyone. It is not simply a wonderful dream. We are being asked to bring about this Kingdom now, which means that somehow we have to find these divine qualities within ourselves.

Faithfulness

Spirituality springs from faith in God and his revealed truth. It is the grace of God and the power of the Spirit, working in our hearts and turning them to God, which enables us to believe and live out our faith. Certainly, no one can **will** themselves to believe: our faith is a gift from God which fills us with immense thankfulness.

Having faith in this 'invisible' God does not imply a cold and rational affair, but an intimate relationship of love. In the Scriptures, we read how God addresses us frequently as his beloved sons and daughters.

The deepest truth about God was revealed to us by Christ. The life of Christ is a mirror in which we see what God is like; and the Holy Spirit is with us always, to lead us to the Father.

As believers, we have to constantly reaffirm our faith, and particularly at times of difficulty.

There can be occasions when we become plagued by doubts and uncertainties; times when we may feel angry with God; and periods of depression or aridity. Then, all we can do is cling on and remain faithful to God in prayer and in religious practice; resisting the tendency to turn our back or run away. Whatever happens, we can be absolutely certain that God remains faithful to us, for he cannot reject his own sons and daughters.

Mercy and Compassion

Mercy in itself is only possible to God. The mercy we show in any given circumstance is only a pale shadow of God's mercy and compassion; but, as such, we are demonstrating a divine attribute.

The infinite power of forgiveness and mercy shown by God towards our sinfulness was won by Christ on the cross. There is no human sin which can prevail over this power or even limit it. Only our obstinacy, or lack of readiness to repent, can limit God's grace and mercy.

Mercy was one of the principle themes of Jesus' preaching. Christ taught that people should be guided in their lives by mercy and forgiveness. In the Sermon on the Mount, he proclaimed: 'Blessed are the merciful, for they shall obtain mercy.'

There are many parables about forgiveness, the most dramatic one being the story of the prodigal son, in which the father's compassion towards his wayward son is the image for all time of God's compassion towards sinners, and a model of how we should behave to those who offend us. At some time, we are all faced with having to forgive another person. We cannot go through life without being hurt or, in our turn, causing others to be hurt. We have, then, to show mercy and receive mercy.

Justice

Justice and mercy are interwoven. Justice alone cannot establish a relationship based on mutual respect. It must be accompanied by love. Justice is concerned with material things, about rights and about equality.

To show our love and concern for people, we have to act justly towards them - whether they are family, employees, tenants, relations, or friends. It is not enough simply to say you love them. People have rights and a need for their personal freedom. The whole of society has an obligation to look after the poor and the needy, and to tackle the social problems which cause injustices between people. The whole civilised world has obligations in justice to the hungry and deprived peoples in different parts of the world. In fighting for these rights, we may have to be challenging and demanding. Seeking after justice does not conflict with our long-term purpose of peace and unity.

We have, also, a personal right to demand justice for ourselves in terms of equality and rights. It requires real wisdom to know how to achieve our individual or group aims, and yet to ensure good communication and relationships. Here, tolerance and respect for human dignity is a sound basis for furthering understanding.

Peace

We often think of peace in terms of absence of conflict or struggle. This is certainly true. But when we speak of peace, we are usually thinking of an ideal world in which all people live in harmony and peace. Perhaps this vision will only be brought to its fullness in the Kingdom to come. In the meantime, we must struggle to bring peace where we can, in our own situation and to the troubled areas of society.

Looking at peace in the context of personal

spirituality, the peace we are seeking is a deep inner peace: a peace which can only be found in the utter conviction that God is with us in every situation.

Whatever the sufferings or difficulties which assail us, we can be certain of this: that we are in God's loving hands. This does not mean that we are not being tossed and pummelled by the things which happen to us; but rather, just as the waves of the sea crash and pound on the surface, and in the deeper depths the water can be still and unaffected by the storm, so it is with us.

As Ronald Rolheiser wrote in the Catholic Herald of 1.3.91:

> We are called to community, to stay with each other. This, despite romantic dreams about friendship, marriage and community, is singularly the most difficult task there is. We cannot ever be close to anyone long without seriously hurting him or her, and she or he seriously hurting us. Hence, community depends upon us having the resilience to forgive, forget, bounce back, and live in some joy and happiness, despite having been hurt and wounded.

Personal Reflection

1. How do I show faithfulness to God and to other people in my life?

2. How do I experience God's forgiveness and compassion? Are there situations in my life when I am called to show mercy and compassion to others?

3. What aspects of justice do I feel most strongly about: in my own life; in society; in the Church; in the world?

4   To what extent have I to admit to some prejudice towards other people (eg ethnic and national groups, the needy, those with a different life-style, etc)?

5   Do I normally reflect my faith in God by showing a positive attitude to the events of life?

Prayer-Time

Preparation: It is suggested that you have some posters depicting needs, eg the third world, poverty at home, peace programmes, anything which brings to mind the theme of this liturgy.

Introduction: Lord, you are full of mercy and love. We come to you today to pray for your grace, so that we may be channels of your love and compassion in the world.

Reading: from John Paul II's encyclical 'This is God's Mercy' para 14

> Conversion in the spirit of mercy
> is a way of life,
> an essential characteristic
> of the Christian vocation.
> It is the day-to-day discovery
> and practice of love,
> as a unifying and uplifting power.
> This is merciful love,
> a creative love.
> In a relationship between persons,
> merciful love is never on only one side;
> when it seems only one is giving
> and the other receiving, ...
> the one who gives also receives,
> also experiences merciful love;
> can also find himself or herself

the object of mercy.

Recite Together: Psalm 84

I will hear what the Lord God has to say,
a voice that speaks of peace,
peace for his people and his friends
and those who turn to him in their hearts.
His help is near for those who fear him
and his glory will dwell in our land.

Mercy and Faithfulness have met;
Justice and Peace have embraced.
Faithfulness shall spring from the earth
and Justice look down from heaven.

The Lord will make us prosper
and our earth shall yield its fruit.
Justice shall march before him
and Peace shall follow his steps.

Reading: From Mechtild of Magdeburg

If you love the justice of Jesus Christ
more than you fear human judgment,
then you will seek to do compassion.

Compassion means
that if I see my friend and my enemy
in equal need,
I shall help both equally.

Justice demands
that we seek
and find the stranger,
the broken, the prisoner,
and comfort them
and offer them our help.

Here lies the holy compassion of God
that causes the devils so much distress.

•

Here, Jesus Christ in union with his Father and with each person, gives us the Spirit who makes us like himself and leads us to the Father. The

Church hungers for the Spirit as it hungers for justice, for peace, love and human dignity.

Recite Together:
>Come Holy Spirit.
>Heal our wounds, our strength renew.
>On our dryness, pour your dew.
>Wash the stains of sin away.
>Bend the stubborn heart and will.
>Melt the frozen, warm the chill.
>Guide the steps that go astray.

Kiss of Peace: This session has been looking at the vision of building up a world of justice, love and peace. As a token of this, we are going to offer one another a sign of peace (or hold hands and sing a suitable song, such as 'Shalom, my friends').

Prayer: from Huub Oosterhuis
>Make us receptive and open
>and may we accept your Kingdom
>like children taking bread
>from the hands of their father.
>Let us live in your peace,
>at home with you
>all the days of our lives. Amen

International Prayer for Peace:
>Lead me from death
>To life, from falsehood to truth.
>
>Lead me from despair
>To hope, from fear to trust.
>
>Lead me from hate
>To love, from war to peace.
>
>Let peace fill our heart,
>Our world, our universe. Amen

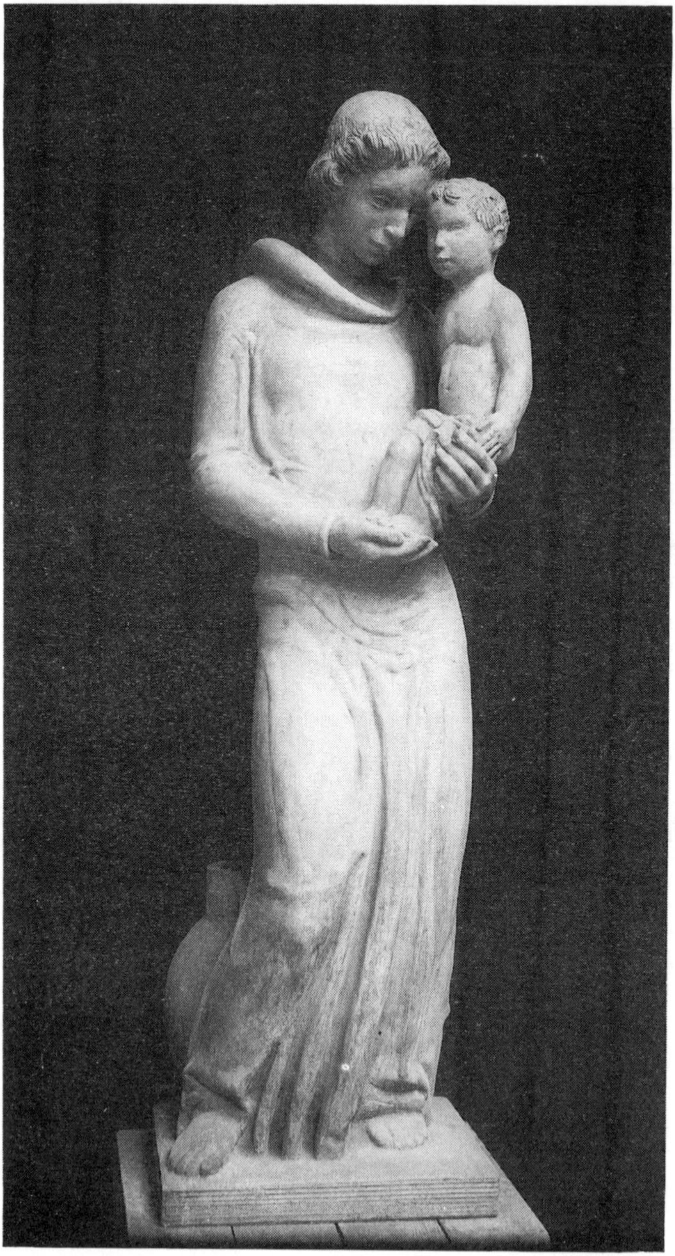

MARY, MOTHER OF THE CHURCH

One of the finest contributions made by the English Bishops at the Second Vatican Council was to stress the importance of placing Mary in her rightful place within the Church. We find the role of Mary defined and affirmed in the most fundamental and profound document of the Council: 'Lumen Gentium' ('This is the Church'). In Chapter 8, it says:

> Mary is rightly honoured
> as Mother of God,
> Mother of the Redeemer.
> She received the Word of God
> in her heart and in her body
> and she gave Life to the world.
> Redeemed by her Son
> in a special manner,
> she is intimately related to him
> with an unbreakable bond.
> To her belongs the dignity of being
> the Mother of God's Son,
> the chosen daughter of the Father,
> the dwelling place of the Spirit.
> On account of this tremendous office
> Mary soars far above all other creatures.
> Even more
> she is truly the mother of the faithful
> because by her love
> she has helped to bring about
> the birth of all
> who are members of the Church.

Mary – Who Said 'YES' To God

The image of Mary as a young girl bowing before

the angel at the annunciation has been the subject of countless paintings and works of art throughout the ages. Its very familiarity makes us forget the overwhelming reality of what was being asked of Mary.

God must have seen, in Mary, a person who had been totally faithful and obedient to his Word throughout her life. Only because of this total acceptance of God's will for her was she able to make her 'fiat' - to say 'Yes'.

In para 21 of 'To Honour Mary' Pope Paul VI says:

> 'I am the handmaid of the Lord.
> Let what you have said be done to me.'
> In these words, she anticipates in herself
> the prayer of Jesus, who said
> 'Your will be done'.
> This 'Yes',
> this 'let it be done' of Mary's,
> is a lesson
> an example of obedience to God's will.
> Such obedience is the way
> that each of us
> will grow in holiness;
> the means that will unite us to God.

Mary, A Woman Of Strength

Popular piety has often depicted Mary as a mild, gentle, and somewhat unworldly creature. The Evangelists do not tell us very much about her but the words spoken by Mary are strong and compelling, and must give living witness of how they experienced her presence. The Magnificat is a song full of exultation and prophetic vision.

We are also given some indication of what Mary had to face and what difficulties she had to overcome. She did not have prior knowledge of the mysterious events which unfolded in her life. She had to meet those extraordinary happenings, and respond with strength and trust. What were her feelings when Jesus left her, to begin his public ministry? Was her faith tested when she saw him preaching and healing, when she heard him speak so intimately about his Father? She must have had increasing anxiety about what was to happen in the end.

She had to live in the present, as we do, and could not know that all would be well in the end. She could only continue to love and unite herself with her Son, and believe that God would be with him.

Again, in para 58 of 'To Honour Mary', we find:

> Thus Mary went forward
> in her pilgrimage of faith
> in close union with her Son
> even to his crucifixion.
> In accordance with God's plan
> she stood at the cross
> suffering with her Son,
> uniting herself to his sacrifice,
> consenting to his immolation.
> And finally, the dying Christ
> gave her as a mother to his disciples
> when he said:
> 'Woman, behold thy son'.

Mary, Who Goes Before Us

Mary was the first follower of Jesus, the first Christian. And we know, for certain, that she is experiencing now the eternal life won for us by the resurrection of Christ and promised to all who follow him. Just as Mary interceded at the marriage feast at Cana, and as she prayed with the apostles and followers of Jesus, so now she continues to pray and intercede for the whole Church, and for each one of us.

Paul VI makes this same point in para 18 of his document:

> Mary's powerful presence

in the early Church
has continued ever since
for, though she has gone to heaven,
she still carries on her mission
of interceding for us
and caring for us.

Personal Reflection

1 How do I see Mary: as mother, friend, model, miracle worker, intercessor?

2 What part does Mary play in my prayer? Do I turn to Mary on specific occasions?

3 Do I make a point of developing my devotion to Mary by saying the rosary, going on pilgrimage, etc.?

4 Which aspect of Mary depicted in the Gospels inspires me most?

5 Mary as a woman gives an image of feminine sanctity. How does this help me to develop my own sexuality in relation to holiness?

Prayer-Time

Preparation: It would be suitable to have an icon or other image of Mary and Child, with a lamp or candle burning, as a focus for this liturgy.

Introduction: Lord, let the gracious intercession of the Blessed Mary, ever virgin, help us. May she guide and protect us, and make us rejoice in your peace. We make our prayer through Christ our Lord.

Reading: from the Book of Judith, Chap 13

O daughter,
you are blessed by the Most High God
above all women on earth;

and blessed be the Lord God
who created the heavens and the earth,
who has guided you
to strike the head
of the leader of our enemies.
Your hope will never depart
from the hearts of men and women,
as they remember the power of God.

Recite Together: **The Magnificat**

My soul glorifies the Lord,
my spirit rejoices in God, my Saviour.

He looks on his servant in her lowliness;
henceforth all ages will call me blessed.

The Almighty works marvels for me.
Holy his name!

His mercy is from age to age
on those who fear him.

He puts forth his arm in strength
and scatters the proud-hearted.

He casts the mighty from their thrones
and raises the lowly.

He fills the starving with good things,
sends the rich away empty.

He protects Israel, his servant,
remembering his mercy,

the mercy promised to our fathers,
for Abraham and his sons for ever.

Reading: From 'To Honour Mary' (para 22)

The Church is filled with wonder,
seeing in Mary
a perfect model
of all that the Church itself
longs and hopes to become.
The Church studies her attentively,
recognising how she is
Christ's associate in the redemption.

The Church sees in Mary
the prophetic fulfilment of its future
as it waits for the day
when, purified from every blemish,
it will become like the Bride
adorned for Christ the Bridegroom.

Litany: by Cardinal Hume

Mary of Bethlehem - Pray for all mothers.
Mary of Nazareth - Pray for all families.
Mary of Cana - Pray for all married couples.
Mary at the Cross - Pray for all who suffer.
Mary in the Upper Room - Pray for all who wait.
Mary, model of womanhood - Pray for all women.

Woman who wondered - Remember us to God.
Woman who listened - Remember us ...
Woman who followed him - Remember us ...
Woman who longed for him - Remember us ...
Woman who loves him - Remember us ...

Further Intercessions, if appropriate

Hymn: from appendix

Final Prayer:

Lord, as we honour the Virgin Mary,
may her faith and love inspire us
to serve you more faithfully in the
work of redemption.

SPIRITUALITY OF SEXUALITY

In the first session, we have emphasised that spirituality is concerned with the whole person. If this is true, then our sexuality - which is so important a part of every human being - must be a channel of grace and holiness.

Becoming Oneself

Our sexuality closely relates to our personal identity, and how we perceive ourselves in relation to others. In becoming the person God wants us to be, and in our praise and worship of him, we grow and develop according to our gender. Being a man or being a woman influences our feelings, relationships, attitudes, actions, communication, and how we view the world and our place in it.

From an early age, we learn the meaning of love through bodily communication: smiles, murmurs of approval, being touched and held. It is by means of this communication that the child discovers self, and learns to get close to people and to communicate. Throughout life, our body is the means by which we receive love and give love - through touch, vision and sound. To aid our growth and capacity to love, we need others to accept and affirm us, allowing us freedom to be ourselves and to live as independent and well-motivated individuals.

For most people, marriage is the means by which they give full expression to their sexuality, both within their intimate sexual life, and also through the interaction of husband and wife in an ongoing and sustained relationship. There is opportunity, in the intimate experience of marriage, for emotional expression, healing of past wounds, the affirming of each other, mutual exchange, and a shared spiritual journey.

All close relationships have some of these elements and, in friendships between men and women, there is the added complementary nature of their interaction and exchange. Celibate and single people are able to direct their sexuality towards many and varied relationships. They also have a freedom to give their time and energy to others in wholehearted love and service.

Roles of Women and Men

The Synod of Bishops devoted much time to the advancement of the role of women in the world and in the church. They felt that women had been discriminated against simply by being women, and there was urgent need to promote women's dignity and equality. The rigid allocation of role to women and men in the past has often been detrimental to both sexes. It has forced both women and men into developing themselves to fit the stereotype role and behaviour expected by our culture. Changes are now taking place, but we must recognise that these changing roles put pressures on communication and relationships between people at all levels.

Feminine and Masculine

Each one of us possesses qualities of the opposite sex. To be a whole person, it is necessary for us to balance the feminine and masculine in ourselves. Undoubtedly, there are basic differences between women and men but, because of cultural views on how each should behave, there is a tendency to develop certain aspects of our own personality, with little opportunity to develop the opposite aspects. We

Love transforms.
Love makes
empty hearts
overflow.
This happens
even more when
we have to
struggle through,
without
assurance,
all unready
for the play
of LOVE.

Mechtilde of Magdeburg

need to work for a society where it is 'all right' for men to show emotion, sensitivity, tenderness, vulnerability; and where women can be rational, strong, assertive, and demonstrate leadership qualities, without being a threat or stepping out of line.

This has wider implications. Because the masculine element has prevailed for so long in Western society, much emphasis in education has been put on the mind, intellect and will. In politics, commerce and industry, the rational, organisational and hierarchical structures have been given high value. There is great need for some contrast here with the reflection of a more feminine, subjective and contemplative approach, where individuals are sustained and nurtured.

Feminine in the Church

If the above is true about society, it is particularly true of the Church.

In the early days of the Church, when the Christian communities were small, it is likely that women and men shared equally in the life of these young churches. As it developed, an institutional pattern of hierarchy emerged, with the power and leadership of the church in the hands of the clergy. It is understandable that largely masculine rational qualities have influenced the institution in such areas as organisation, dogma, law, order, discipline, etc.

This needs to be balanced by a more person-centred, nurturing, intuitive, and sensitive approach. More involvement of women in church affairs will not necessarily bring this about, unless everyone sees it as a need.

Both priests and laity - men and women - have to allow the feminine to be more freely expressed in the life, liturgy and prayer of the church. The creative gifts of the people of God should be freely made use of. The development and use of music, dance, myth and drama in Christian education, as well as an openness and sensitivity to different movements and needs in the church, should all be encouraged.

Personal Reflection

1   Do I find it possible to address God as 'Mother'? What difference would it make in my image of God? Does it help my prayer?

2   How do I express my sexuality? Do I see it as a God-given gift which brings me in touch with his divine life?

3   What are my relations with the opposite sex:
    * with people who are close to me?
    * with work colleagues?
    * or with people whom I meet in various situations?

4   Do I view the opposite sex with openness, or am I conditioned by past experiences, prejudices, resentments and anger, which make it difficult for me to communicate?

5   Which 'feminine' qualities am I able to express in my life?

Prayer-Time

Preparation: No obvious visual aid springs to mind for this liturgy, other than recognising that those men and women present represent their own symbol as they come together to celebrate and thank God for their humanity.

However, someone may have an object or representation which symbolises wholeness or harmony, or the inter-relatedness of opposites eg the mandala, which would be entirely appropriate as a centre-piece.

Introduction: Come, Holy Spirit, and bring us your strength. Open our hearts so that we may be more generous in our relationships, more willing to let others be different, and ourselves able to grow in love and compassion.

Reading: from 1st Letter of John, Ch 4: 7-12

> Let us love one another;
> for love is of God,
> and anyone who loves is born of God
> and knows God.
> Those who do not love, do not know God;
> for God is love.
> In this, the love of God
> was made manifest among us:
> that God sent his only Son into the world,
> so that we might live through him.
> In this is love:
> not that we loved God,
> but that he loved us,
> and sent his Son
> to be the expiation for our sins.
> If God so loved us,
> we also ought to love one another.
> No one has ever seen God;
> if we love one another,
> God abides in us
> and his love is perfected in us.

Recite Together: Psalm 8 which praises God for our humanity.

> How great is your name, O Lord our God,
> through all the earth.

> Your majesty is praised above the heavens;
> on the lips of children and of babes
> you have found praise to foil your enemy,
> to silence the foe and the rebel.

> When I see the heavens,

the work of your hands,
the moon and the stars which you arranged,
what are we that you should keep us in mind,
men and women, that you care for us?

Yet you have made us little less than gods,
and crowned us with glory and honour,
gave us power over the works of your hands,
put all things under our feet.

All of them, sheep and cattle,
yes, even the savage beasts,
birds of the air, and fish
that make their way through the waters.

How great is your name, O Lord our God,
through all the earth.

Reading: from 'The Marriage of East and West' by Bede Griffiths, OSB

God looks out upon the contemporary world with an unwavering faith, for he sees in it a wealth of initially diverse movements ultimately destined to converge.

There was the holistic movement, the ecological movement, the feminine movement. It was of vital importance that people discovered the feminine in their lives; and linked to this was the peace movement, for in a world driven on by the masculine, dominating energy, conflict was inevitable.

Only the rediscovery of the feminine could bring peace. There was a movement towards the recognition of sexuality in spiritual life, the acknowledgement that celibacy was a paricular calling, but that marriage - the union of the masculine and feminine - was the usual and valid way to God.

·

God is not only fatherly,

God is also mother
who lifts her loved child
from the ground to her knee.

The Trinity is like a mother's cloak
wherein the child finds a home
and lays its head on the maternal breast.

> Mechtild of Magdeburg

Reading: from 'This is the Laity' (para 52)

The fundamental reason why women and men
should collaborate is because
this is part of God's original plan.
He willed the human being
to be 'a unity of two'.
He willed women and men to be
the primary community of persons,
the source of all other communities.
At the same time, he willed them
to be a 'sign'
of the interpersonal community of love
which is the life of the Trinity.

Silence - during which we can pray for more understanding and collaboration between women and men.

Bidding Prayers

Hymn: from Appendix

Final Prayer:

O God, may the fire of the Holy Spirit
burn up the dross in our hearts,
warm them with love
and set them on fire
with zeal for your service.

GOD IS
NOT ONLY
FATHERLY;
GOD IS ALSO MOTHER

Mechtilde of Magdeburg

APPENDIX A

WAYS INTO PRAYER

* Close your eyes, and become silent by letting go of all the tensions in your body. Concentrate on your breathing and let it help you to become quiet. Let your body remain upright and attentive, and gradually allow all the tensions and pressures of the day to disappear. When you have this inner silence, and feel centred within yourself, simply remain like this in God's presence.

* Choose a text from Scripture, or take the reading from the Morning or Evening Prayer of the Church. Allow one word or one phrase to speak to you. Grow still, and become aware of your own response to this particular passage. This may lead you to reflect on aspects of your life, about which you can then pray.

* Alternatively, you can simply take the word or phrase you have chosen and repeat it slowly and quietly and use it like a mantra, not thinking about its meaning but using it simply as a means of remaining attentive to God within you. Each time you are distracted, repeat the phrase or word without hurry or anxiety.

* Some people take a word such as 'Abba' or 'Jesus' and use it to repeat over and over again. Similarly, the Jesus Prayer has been used in this way by Christians for hundreds of years: 'Lord Jesus Christ, Son of God, have mercy upon me, a sinner.' Say this prayer as you breathe out, and you will get into a peaceful rhythm. The rosary is often used in a similar fashion, as a background prayer.

* At times of great difficulty or emotional stress, it is sometimes impossible to put feelings and anxieties to one side. Then, it is best to sit before God in silence and to pour out to him all our feelings, in the sure knowledge that he understands our emotions, however unruly and negative they may be. In this way, we can express our trust and belief in his everlasting love and compassion for us.

* If these situations involve personal hurt and injury, and we come to prayer with feelings of anger and resentment, it is no good pretending that we are not feeling these emotions. Our prayer must surely include accepting our feelings, and asking God for his grace to help us to cope, and to show us what can be done about it.

* In places of natural beauty, we can allow the wonder and beauty of creation to lead us to prayers of thanksgiving and praise.

* Simply expressing prayers of love, adoration, thanksgiving, petition.

* Prayers of petition which spring from our own needs, and the needs of the world. Taking a newspaper, and using this as a means of expressing our concern for the society in which we live, is a good way of making our prayer relevant and concerned with the real world. Try to imagine what Jesus would think if he read our daily newspaper.

* Photographs, images, paintings may help us into prayer. Gaze at these objects, and allow them to touch your inner longings and help to lead you into prayer.

* Similarly, music can create an atmosphere, and touch the imagination and feelings in such a way that it is easy to turn to God, or just enjoy the music in his presence.

APPENDIX B

These quotations supplement the material in the following sessions. They can be used for meditation on the particular theme, or a copy given to each person, in a group, to use at home.

SPIRITUALITY OF THE LAITY

Our prayer is God's work, God's creation.
As you kneel there,
sit there, walk about
or whatever you do when you pray,
you are saying 'Yes' with your whole being
to His will that you should be,
that you should be you,
that you should be united to Him.

Becoming Prayer
Maria Boulding OSB

NETWORK OF RELATIONSHIPS

Each family is a tiny nation:
and like nations,
each family, each household,
should have its own set
of folk customs and traditions:
special foods,
special activities on certain feast days.
All combine to form a living,
personal, family tradition.
These domestic traditions
need to be simple but real;
joyful and not superficially pious;
prayerful and playful,
so that they will nourish
all the members of the family.

Prayers for the Domestic Church
Ed Hayes

IN THE DARKNESS

Love transforms.
Love makes empty hearts overflow.
This happens even more
when we have to struggle through
without assurance,
all unready for the play of Love.

                          Mechtild of Magdeburg

CREATION SPIRITUALITY

The incarnation is a making new,
a restoration
of all the universe's forces and powers;
Christ is the instrument,
the Centre, the End,
of the whole animate and material creation;
Through Him everything is created,
sanctified and vivified.

                          Prayer of the Universe
                          Teilhard de Chardin

PERSONAL JOURNEY

The story to which you listen in Scripture
and your own life as you live it
are mutually illuminating:
you can hear the word in Scripture
because you know the hidden word in your life,
but it is the scriptural word
which is a lamp for your steps
and a light for your path
as you go back again to the task of living.

                          The coming of God
                          Maria Boulding OSB

EVANGELISATION

We are caught up in the paradox, the mystery of the indwelling of God in our lives. He is the stranger dying in the gutter, the deranged

Rumanian toddler bashing his head against the bars of his cot; but he is also the Samaritan lifting up our broken bodies, and the gentle paediatrician clasping us, weeping and soiled, in his arms. What more need we know? He is there, in it, with us, in us, over and under, inside and out, a cloud of unkowing, a shield to defend us.

Sheila Cassidy

APPENDIX C

SUGGESTED HYMNS

This is a list of suggested hymns and songs for each Section. The first line is given and the number in brackets refers to 'Hymns Old & New' published by Kevin Mayhew.

LAY LIFE

Breathe on me, Breath of God   (70)
Christ be beside me   (79)
Father I place into your hands   (133)
Take my hands   (509)
Walk with me, Oh my Lord   (582)

SPIRITUALITY OF WORK

Fear not, rejoice and be glad   (137)
I give my hands to do your work   (235)
Lord of all hopefulness   (329)
Seek ye first the Kingdom of God   (473)

NETWORK OF RELATIONSHIPS

A new commandment I give unto you (39)
Bind us together, Lord   (62)
Feed us now, O Son of God   (138)
O, let all who thirst   (400)
Where is love & loving-kindness   (615)
Taize: Ubi Caritas

IN THE DARKNESS

Do not be afraid   (122)
Jesus, you are Lord   (286)
Lay your hands gently upon us   (295)
Now the green blade riseth   (376)

The light of Christ   (529)
You shall cross the barren desert   (627)

PRAYER

All the earth proclaim the Lord   (29)
Be still and know that I am God   (58)
Keep in mind   (290)
Spirit of the Living God   (501)
Taize: O Lord hear my prayer
Psalm 62   Grail/Gelineau   (638)

CREATION SPIRITUALITY

All   Creation bless the Lord   (9)
All creatures of our God and King   (10)
All the nations of the earth   (30)
O praise ye the Lord!   (425)
Psalm 8   Grail/Gelineau   (629)
Psalm 144   Grail Gelineau   (659)

PERSONAL JOURNEY

I will be with you wherever you go   (263)
Oh, the word of my Lord, deep within   (431)
The love I have for you, my Lord   (536)
This is my will, my one command   (557)
Yahweh, I know you are near   (620)
Psalm 90   Grail/Gelineau   (643)

EVANGELISATION

Colours of day dawn into the mind   (87)
Do you know that the Lord walks on earth (124)
Fear not, rejoice and be glad   (137)
Look around you, can you see   (316)

JUSTICE AND MERCY

Forth in the peace of Christ we go   (147)
How lovely on the mountains   (224)
Peace is flowing like a river   (442)
Seek ye first the Kingdom of God   (473)
Psalm 71   Grail/Gelineau   (640)

MARY - MOTHER OF THE CHURCH

As I kneel before you   (45)
Holy virgin, by God's decree   (218)
Tell out my soul   (514)
Where are you bound, Mary, Mary   (614)
The Magnificat   Grail/Gelineau   (661)

SPIRITUALITY OF SEXUALITY

I watch the sunrise lighting the sky   (262)
I will never forget you, my people   (265)
Love is his word   (338)
My love for you will never leave you   (362)
Psalm 127   Grail/Gelineau   (654)

This list does not aim to be comprehensive. Many of the hymns found here are also suitable for occasions other than the one given here.

ACKNOWLEDGEMENTS

Every effort has been made to trace copyright material and we hope that no copyright has been infringed. If, however, infringements have occurred, corrections will be made in any reprints of this book.

*

The Grail is grateful for permission to reproduce the following copyright material:

'Called to Become'
from 'Psalms of a Laywoman' by Edwina Gateley.
Publisher: Anthony Clarke, Hemel Hempstead.

'Be born in us...' page 31
by Caryll Houselander.
Copyright: Sheed and Ward

'I am thinking of the commandment...' page 40
from 'To be a Pilgrim by Cardinal Basil Hume OSB
St Paul Publications

'The life of prayer, the life of ...' page 46
from 'Prayer' by Abhishiktananda
(Henri le Saux OSB)
Publisher: SPCK

'Lord Jesus Christ...' page 83
from 'Contemporary Prayers for Public Worship'
edited by Caryl Micklem.
SCM Press 1967

'God looks out upon ...' page 105
Copyright 1982 Bede Griffiths, from Marriage of East and West
Published by Collins

'Each family is a tiny nation:...' page 110
from 'Prayers for the Domestic Church'
by Rev Ed Hayes
Published by Shantivanam House of Prayer, Easton, Kansas 66020

'We are caught up in the paradox...' page 111
from _Good Friday People_ by Sheila Cassidy
Publisher: Darton, Longman & Todd

Reprinted from _Meditations with Meister Eckhart_
edited by Matthew Fox
copyright 1983 Bear & Co., by permission of Bear & Co., Inc., PO Drawer 2860, Santa Fe, NM 87504, the following:
'We are fellow helpers with God...' page 32

Reprinted from _Original Blessing_ by Matthew Fox,
copyright Bear & Co Inc. 1983, by permission of Bear and Co., Inc., PO Drawer 2860, Santa Fe, NM 87504, the following:
'Facing the darkness,...' page 58

Reprinted from _Meditations with Julian of Norwich_ edited by Brendan Doyle,
copyright 1983 Bear & Co., by permission of Bear & Co., Inc., PO Drawer 2860, Santa Fe, NM 87504, the following:
'I saw for certain...' page 40
'God feels great delight...' page 42
'There is a treasure...' page 67

Reprinted from _Meditations with Mechtild of Magdeburg_, edited by Sue Woodruff,
Copyright 1982 Bear & Co., Inc., by permission of Bear & Co., Inc., PO Drawer 2860, Santa Fe, NM 87504, the following:
'If you love the justice...' page 90
'Love transforms, Love...',,page 101 & 111
'God is not only fatherly...' page105/6

Reprinted from _Meditations with Hildegard of Bingen_, edited by Gabriel Uhlein,
Copyright 1983 Bear & Co. Inc., by permission of Bear & Co. Inc., PO Drawer 2860, Santa Fe, NM 87504, the following:
'God has created me...' page 73

All Scripture quotations are taken from the Revised Standard Version
Published by Collins
Copyright: Division of Christian Education of the National Council of the Churches of Christ in the USA – Old Testament 1952
New Testament 1946

The Grail (England) owns the following copyrights:

All Psalm quotations are from:
The Grail Psalms: An Inclusive Version
Publisher: Collins

Extracts from Council & other Vatican Documents are taken from Grail simplifications of:

This is the Laity (Christifideles Laici)

This is the Church (Lumen Gentium)

This is God's Mercy (Dives et Misericordia)

This is Human Work (Laborem Exercens)

To Honour Mary (Marialis Cultus) taken from:
'With Mary into the Third Millennium'

'Lord Jesus, I give you my hands...' page 21 the Grail Prayer

BIBLIOGRAPHY

Apart from those listed in the acknowledgments, the following books were also used as resource material:

Becoming Prayer
Jean-Pierre Dubois-Dumee
Publisher: St Paul Publications

Markings
Dag Hammerskjöld
Publisher: Faber

Experimental Liturgy Book
Robert Hoey
Publisher: Crossroad Books

Cosmic Christ
Teilhard de Chardin
Publisher: Fontana

The Coming of God
Maria Boulding OSB
Publisher SPCK

Your Word is Near
Huub Oosterhuis
Publisher: Newman Press

GRAIL PUBLICATIONS

THIS IS THE CHURCH
Grail simplification of 'Lumen Gentium'. This may be regarded as **the** masterpiece of Vatican II. Read this and find how it enlarges your vision of the Church.   £2.75

THE CHURCH IN THE WORLD TODAY
Grail simplification of 'Gaudium et Spes'. An essentially 'pastoral' document which is an eye-opener on the role of Christians in today's swiftly changing scene. A Vatican II document. £3.50

THIS IS GOD'S MERCY
Grail version of 'Dives et Misericordia'. In the tensions of today, caused largely by world-wide inequalities, the Church must bear true witness, says John Paul II.   £1.75

THIS IS HUMAN WORK
Grail simplification of 'Laborem Exercens'. Pope John Paul deals with capital and labour, worker's rights and the spiritualisation of work. 85p

THIS IS THE LAITY
A simplification of 'Christifideles Laici'.'This will help to guide the Church into the next century.' It is meant for all Christians: young, old, well-known, obscure, handicapped or sick. It deals positively with the role of women, conservation, the need for re-evangelisation and the rise of new groups within the Church.   £3.00

WITH MARY INTO THE THIRD MILLENNIUM
A pack presenting notes, readings, prayers and discussion material. Also containing specially simplified extracts from Pope Paul VI's document 'To Honour Mary'. Suitable for groups, personal study or schools.   £3.00

THE GRAIL PSALMS
A translation made from the Hebrew and put into powerful, plain English. The three versions are all published by Collins Liturgical Publications:

Text Only Intended for private reading and prayer, this has become the favourite version of thousands of Christians.   £2.95

Singing Version This allows us to use the Psalms as their original users did, namely to sing them. Rhythmic accents for each line are indicated, and the musical formulas of Joseph Gelineau are given.   £3.50

Inclusive Language Version A version based on the original translation. This is welcomed by those who find the language of many of the psalms excessively masculine.   £3.95

If you would like to receive a catalogue of all Grail Publications, please write to:

> Grail Publications
> 125 Waxwell Lane
> Pinner, Middx   HA5 3ER

Please send any orders to the distributors:
> GRACEWING (Fowler Wright)
> Unit 2, Southern Avenue
> Leominster, Herefords HR6 0QF

THE GRAIL

The Grail is a Society, part of which is a Secular Institute for women. The Centre is at Pinner, Middlesex.

The Grail Centre is the home of a group of Christian women who have made a long term commitment to a simple life-style, to helping individuals grow, to building community and to caring for the earth on a small scale. Others, men and women, sharing this ethos and the work that flows from it, become part of the community for longer or shorter periods of time. Some community members run the Centre.

The Grail is well-known for its publications, in particular, for the Grail translation of the Psalms and for the simplifications of many Vatican documents. Extracts from these are used in this publication.

The Grail is constantly changing. The work undertaken is a response to reading the signs of the times and responding to the promptings of the Holy Spirit.

At the Centre, the Grail offers people space for peace and quiet, a chance to 'get away from it all'. They come from all walks of life, and we enable them to discover a new way of re-creating themselves.

Within the Grail there is room for anyone sharing their ideals and vision. If you would like further information about their life, work or publications, write to:

Mary Grasar
The Grail Centre, 125 Waxwell Lane
Pinner, Middx HA5 3ER